DESIGN YOUR LAW PRACTICE

Using Design Thinking to Get Next Level Results

Jessica Bednarz, Catherine Sanders Reach,
and Juda Strawczynski, Editors

AMERICAN BAR ASSOCIATION
Law Practice Division

Cover design by Amanda Fry/ABA Design

Printed in the United States of America.

27 26 25 24 23 5 4 3 2 1

ISBN: 978-1-63905-259-2
e-ISBN: 978-1-63905-260-8

A catalog record for this book is available from the Library of Congress.

Contents

2

3

PART II
Putting It All Together

PART III
Real World Examples

Foreword

Jess Birken

I've given a lot of CLE lately, which means I have the chance to hear how other people introduce me. Lately, the person introducing me will usually say I'm an "innovator" in my law practice (I serve small nonprofits, so, think: small business law plus some extra compliance on the side).

Innovator—it's got a nice ring to it! And it's a great compliment, but it's not quite true.

I'll agree that I am *weird* as far as lawyers go. I don't usually do things "the way they've always been done." I run my firm using a Frankenstein's-monster patchwork of no-code tech systems. And, yes, there aren't a ton of lawyers doing *exactly* what I'm doing. I run a firm solely on a subscription service, where I combine flat fee project work for clients and self-help products for other nonprofits.

But . . . innovator? Me? No.

When it comes down to it, I'm not that different from all the lawyers who show up to the CLE talks I give. At those sessions, I'm surrounded by smart, curious lawyers who want to learn something new and improve their practices. I don't have any super-secret knowledge or unique experience they don't have. Yes, I've combined software and business sector things with legal practice things in new ways. But I haven't invented anything *new*.

The only thing that separates me from those other lawyers is execution. Folks come to these CLEs ready to learn, yay! Yet, I rarely hear from them about what they're actually implementing. And, look, I get it—taking the leap from learning to implementing is totally the hard part. It usually takes time, effort, and money. Just the thing all of us overworked lawyers want to do, right?

That's been true for me, for sure. In the process of building the practice I have today, I've used a lot of time trying more software than you can shake a stick at. I've experienced the painful part of that hockey stick shaped learning curve (you know the bottom where all the effort is) more times than most people. I've made mistakes—so many. I've lost some money—not a lot, but enough to learn a few painful lessons. Basically, I've been willing to fail, get knocked down, feel stupid, and get back up and try again. A lot!

What REALLY Holds Lawyers Back

I think what *really* holds most of us back from making *real* change in our law practice isn't about what we need to learn, or the ethics rules. It's more about the fear. Change is really scary and full of unknowns. Here's a pretty common thought scenario from my head when I was just dipping a toe in the waters of change:

> *What will my clients think?. . .*
>
> *Will this even work?. . .*
>
> *What if I get in trouble with the ethics board!?*
>
> *OMG I could go broke.*
>
> *What if this is just a waste of time?*
>
> *What if I choose this and it's the wrong strategy?!*
>
> *I'm not sure I have time for this right now since I'm late on the Jones file. They're going to email me any day now, ack.*
>
> *Maybe I need to hire a consultant instead?*

Maybe that all sounds familiar? I don't know about you, but those unknowns and internal cross-examinations are the silent killers for me. My little hamster-wheel brain starts turning over the risks and what-ifs, and pretty soon the whole thing just seems really overwhelming and intimidating. And heyyyy . . . wasn't there a new season of that show I love on Netflix, maybe I should just see how many episodes are new, and go back to what feels safe and comfortable . . . and then? My inertia grinds to a halt. It's over.

Why does that happen!?

Well, usually we think of change as BIG. We need to COMPLETELY and TOTALLY OVERHAUL the ENTIRE law practice and the way I live my lawyer-life. We have to throw EVERYTHING in the garbage and start living our shiny NEW law-life TODAY!

Who wouldn't be overwhelmed by that? That's nuts!

Make Change in Small Steps

The truth is, though, I really didn't get dropped onto the scene here as fully formed #legaltech super-user who has it all figured out. I promise. That's not me. Not. At. All.

This all started when I decided enough was *enough* with paper files. We're in the 21st century, dang it! It was time to go digital. I convinced my then law partner we should use cloud-based practice management software (Clio). Then I convinced them we should stop using paper and put client files in Dropbox. Then I connected the files to Clio. This alone was a small but still Herculean task—if you have a partner and a server closet, then you know the struggle is real!

I had identified a major problem: maintaining paper files was inconvenient, kept me tied to the physical office, wasn't environmentally friendly, and so on. And then I came up with the solution to the problem (Clio and Dropbox). It wasn't about "innovating." It was about making my lawyer-life better. Just stop losing stuff, stop late night runs to the office for a file, just make life easier, and so on.

Then I up and left my firm and started all over with Birken Law Office (can you say change and upheaval? LOL). I was building my practice again from the ground up—which meant I could try *all* the things. But even then, I started small. For example, I saw someone using online scheduling software, and I thought that would be a great way to manage *my* networking calendar. But I didn't like the way they used it, they made me feel bad . . . like they were *very* important (read: a jerk) and I was a lowly peon that had to do it their way. I didn't like that part.

So, I started doing free trials of a few online scheduling programs. I liked the user interface of Acuity Scheduling. It was easy and made sense. Then I thought about how I could use it and still be friendly, what would I say in my email when I asked people to use it so they didn't feel bad like I had. What words did I want on the scheduling page, and so on. I started a soft launch trying it out. At first, I only tried it with networking meetings. I was too scared to try it on clients (see the list of what ifs).

With this little experiment on my networking lunches and coffees I learned—it was awesome! It cut down on the endless emailing back and forth about availability, and it made it easy and convenient for folks I was trying to network with. All I had to do was send them a link, and then we were set. It was an obvious win-win! As I kept experimenting, I refined the process more and more, tweaked my words and confirmation emails, things like that to improve the experience for me—and for them.

Once I got to know the tool, I started to see *all* the different ways it could improve my practice. So, I decided to try it with clients. I would tell people "I'm trying this new thing, let me know what you think." I got amazing feedback—clients LOVED it so much! Pretty soon, it made sense to schedule *everything* that way, networking lunches to client meetings, and even new client consultations.

Because I had built up my confidence in the tool and how much people liked it, I was less scared to try it for paid consultations. Acuity made it so easy. I could take payment directly at the time of booking through the platform. That made it painless to collect a small fee and not have it rattle around my AR forever. It also made it easy to issue a refund if needed. Clients could easily read the terms of the limited scope engagement letter I baked into the booking process. Then they easily signed it and got a copy with their confirmation email. They could quickly and easily cancel or reschedule without needing to email me about it.

Even better, I had advance notice of who was coming in and could ask a few questions on an intake form that helped me run a conflicts check in Clio before the meeting. In the blink of an eye and all on the right side of the ethics rules! All of these things previously would have felt overwhelming (new technology, trying limited scope, trying something outside the norm for lawyers). But thanks to my little experiment and building on bit by bit, this came pretty easy. (Ok I admit I had my ethics counsel hold my hand a little to review the engagement letter!)

If you were to look at my progress in growing Birken Law Office over the past five years, you'd see this trajectory repeated over and over again. I try something new, just a little experiment—maybe it will work and maybe it won't. I get feedback in real time. And from there, I make more and more small tweaks to make things even better and pretty soon it's a BIG different thing.

In case you think that was a one-off lucky strike, here's another example. After my first adventures with Acuity, I heard about this thing called Zapier that could connect Clio to other programs I used online. At the same time, I'd been thinking "you know, I should have a website that doesn't suck." So I made that happen (with some help—remember I can't code!). In the process of creating the new website I found out I could add my Acuity Scheduling to the site really easily. I tried that. It worked! So then I tried this Zapier program and guess what? I found out I could take the contact information collected by Acuity and use Zapier to (basically) copy it into my MS365 Outlook contacts as a new contact (or update an old contact). My Outlook contacts synced to Clio. Now that's time saved! I was hot to connect everything I could, so I started building more "zaps" with Zapier connecting my online programs to share information between them. If the zaps didn't work, it was no big deal to turn it off or fix it. Each one was a little experiment that I learned from and iterated on.

I built up so much confidence trying zaps that I decided to go a little bigger and try making a short online course for the people I meet with who wanted to start a new nonprofit. I typically give the same speeches over and over to new nonprofit founders, so why not automate that too?!

Then I started tinkering even more with limited scope services, then flat fees, and then I built a subscription program. Now my whole firm has ditched hourly billing and does things in a very different way.

If that sounds like a lot, rest assured it is! That was a multi-year process, and I'm nowhere near done yet.

I don't say all of this to scare you off; quite the opposite. This whole journey was not some linear process, perfectly planned and then flawlessly executed. I just identified problems in my practice (problems for me and problems for the clients). Then I made (mostly small) adjustments along the way to solve for those problems. And taken all together, it added up to real, substantial change for my lawyer-life today.

How to Get Started *Right Now*

Are you hearing me on this yet? You don't need to do everything today or even this year! Whatever you're planning, I'm totally stoked for you. Dream big, have big ideas—that part is fun!

And then, you have to *DO*. You must execute.

On something.

It's easy to get stuck in the dreaming and planning phase. But your dreams and plans *don't* actually mean any real change. At a certain point, you have to roll up your sleeves and get started.

As you get over your fear and get ready to execute, narrow down your first step to the smallest possible chunk. When you think you've made it as small as possible, try making it even smaller still. Trust me, I've learned this lesson over and over again. Even the small things are hard when you're just getting started on a new idea. And we tend to think too big. There are just so many unknown unknowns. So set yourself up for an easier win and get some momentum in your big plans.

In this book we will introduce a methodology for how to move past the way you've always done it and get things done differently by applying design thinking.

You'll learn valuable lessons building that first bit, whatever it is. It doesn't have to be earth shattering.

And you *will* make mistakes, too. It can't be helped! But if you've narrowed down that first step, your mistakes will be small, and you won't have to worry about the big what-ifs (well not as much anyway). The best part? You'll be able to apply what you learn to the next thing, and it will be a little bit easier. Pretty soon, you'll build up a *ton* of knowledge about what works for you (and what doesn't), and a whole lotta confidence along the way. You won't see it as a risk to try new things and experiment even more.

In fact, these days, it's almost more of a risk to keep things exactly the same.

Pretty soon you'll be *weird* like me, combining old things in new ways to serve your community better. And, heck, maybe one day we'll be on the same CLE panel together. They'll call us "innovators" and we'll share little a wink.

Introduction

Jessica Bednarz, Catherine Sanders Reach, and Juda Strawczynski

Welcome to *Design Your Law Practice: A Practical Guide to Design Thinking for Lawyers Looking to Get Things Done.* As the title suggests, this book introduces lawyers and other legal professionals to design thinking as a process that can help implement change in legal practices and the legal system.

As Jess Birken highlights in the Foreword, legal professionals can be overcome by fear. Despite wanting to change, we are at times paralyzed, afraid of making mistakes, of taking whatever we already have, regardless of how imperfect it may be, and making things worse.

This cautious approach is taught starting on day one of law school. Lawyers are trained to look back to precedent before moving forward, and only incrementally advance where permitted. Lawyers are trained to see risk.

While these traditional skills help make excellent trusted legal advisors, other skills are needed for lawyers to build thriving practices, build solutions that meet the needs of their clients, and help reform legal systems so they are accessible for all. Lawyers can also use different skills to not only see risk but also manage it.

Design thinking is the topic of this book. It's one of the skill sets that can help lawyers in all aspects of their practices. It's a field that lawyers can embrace to move forward and get results.

Origins of Design Thinking

Design thinking is widely applied in other sectors, including the automotive, banking, consumer goods, health care, hospitality/tourism, and tech industries.

Design thinking has similarly been applied in the legal services sectors. It is embraced, or is starting to be adapted by:

- **Legal technology companies:** Computer scientists and other professionals have been immersed in user experience (UX), user interface (UI), beta testing, and continuous improvement from day one. (Jack Newton, CEO and Co-Founder of Clio Legal Software contributed a chapter to this book.)
- **Law schools and universities:** In the 2010s, design was starting to be taught in law schools. Margaret Hagan, Executive Director of the Legal Design Lab at Stanford University, is among the pioneers in the field, bringing design thinking into the classroom to solve access to justice challenges, working with justice system partners to make the justice system more accessible and user friendly, and researching how access to justice innovations can be scaled. Metropolitan Toronto University's Legal Innovation Zone (LIZ) works with lawyers, law students, and a range of others to help drive legal innovation, and houses the world's first legal tech incubator. (The LIZ program co-founders contributed a chapter to this book.)
- **Bar associations:** Local, state, and national bar associations are using design thinking to help develop innovative law firms and products. The Chicago Bar Foundation Justice Entrepreneurs Project (JEP) is a small business incubator that helps lawyers launch socially conscious and innovative law firms targeting the underserved middle market.

  (Book co-editor Jessica Bednarz was previously the Associate Director of Innovation & the JEP until January 2023.) The ABA's Center for Innovation has similarly applied design thinking to address some of the most challenging problems facing lawyer regulation and legal service delivery. Among its innovation efforts it has launched its Redesigning Legal Speaker Series, which has provided a new means of considering some of the more seemingly intractable problems around lawyer regulation.

- **Courts, tribunals, and other justice system participants:** Design thinking is being used to reform our justice systems to focus on end-user justice system participants. Governments, the judiciary, and court staff are turning to design thinking approaches to consider reforms to make it easier for people to access services. As one example, British Columbia's Civil Resolution Tribunal (CRT) is an online tribunal offering online dispute-resolution services. The CRT was built based on user needs, and has adopted five guiding principles: that dispute resolution services must be timely, flexible, accessible, affordable, and efficient. The CRT regularly reports on its outcomes, and is committed to continuous improvement. (Contributors Meredith Brown and Sarah McCoubrey regularly work with justice system participants applying design thinking approaches to address challenges in our justice systems.)
- **Law firms:** Some law firms have used design thinking as a leading methodology to help create novel solutions for clients and improve internal knowledge management and processes. (Ginevra Saylor, Director, Innovation and Knowledge Programs at Gowling WLG provides a case study.)

Design thinking can be used by lawyers and law firms to:

- Better understand client needs and use that information as the starting point for solution and process development
- Reduce the risks with launching new products and services
- Allow lawyers, law firms, and our legal system to learn and iterate faster to meet legal needs

Design thinking principles are universal and can help legal professionals in whatever issue or pain point they are trying to address. Before editing this book, we had each been fortunate to use design thinking principles in different ways. We had, for example:

- Assisted attorneys to develop their practices from scratch using design thinking approaches
- Helped attorneys identify key client pain points, and design practical solutions

- Provided feedback as "users" to others using design thinking to develop practice resources and practice management solutions for lawyers
- Used design thinking processes to help implement regulatory reforms aimed at protecting consumers
- Participated in legal design sprints to develop new justice system and court-based approaches to unmet legal needs.

At its core, design thinking is a *mindset*, and an *approach, method,* or *process* for creative problem solving. At its core, design thinking is:

- Focused on the end user/client and rooted in empathy
- Hands-on/practical
- Action-oriented
- Iterative, challenging us to continuously improve

The five steps of the design thinking process are:

1. Empathize/research your user's needs
2. Define—state your user's needs and problems
3. Ideate—how to solve the problem
4. Prototype—start to create solutions
5. Test and refine—try your solutions out and make adjustments based on feedback

The principles in this book can be used by lawyers to improve their practices, regardless of firm size, location, or area of practice. It can be used to build thriving law practices, develop new legal products, find new solutions to unmet legal needs, and help build our future justice systems.

For this book, we have invited different authors to write about each of these five steps. In the following chapters, you'll hear about each step in greater detail.

1. For step 1, empathy, Jack Newton, CEO and Co-Founder of Clio, and author of *The Client-Centered Law Firm*, describes the importance of empathy as the core of the design thinking process. Based on his years building a leading practice management software for lawyers and law offices, Newton describes how the shift to putting yourself in your client's shoes, and practicing deep empathy, can

help lawyers greatly improve how they serve clients, and continuously improve and grow their practices.

2. For step 2, defining your user's needs, Sarah McCoubrey and Meredith Brown, both from Calibrate, build on their years working in and with governments, not-for-profit organizations, and others on legal systems reforms to review how the definition stage requires careful attention to detail. Building the problem statement from the client experience requires lawyers to check biases, actively listen to clients, use their insights to build a draft problem statement, and work to refine it.
3. For step 3, ideation, Lori Gonzalez, CEO/Founder of RayNa Corp, challenges lawyers to stretch past their traditional training, to engage in creative brainstorming sessions with a diverse group of participants. Gonzalez provides practical tips for how to maximize opportunities to get the most out of brainstorming to find new ideas and potential new solutions.
4. For step 4, prototyping, Hersh Perlis and Chris Bentley from Metropolitan Toronto University's Legal Innovation Zone, take lessons learned from working with legal tech startups to share tips to get the most out of this step. Prototyping can be used to build a new product, but can just as easily be used to build or enhance services. They emphasize that prototyping is as much an approach with a purpose as it is creating a thing. They note that prototyping need not be an expensive proposition; the complexity and cost of this stage will depend on the project. Regardless, it's a key step that helps to test proposed solutions, and quickly iterate.
5. For step 5, legal techpreneur, lawyer, and innovator Mary Juetten, CEO of Tracklight.com and the Managing Partner of Singular Law Group PLLC, describes how the testing and refining stage can give key insights into whether what you have developed meets your user's needs, and what further changes could help. She also shares key tips on how to manage this stage to maximize buy-in and the chances of success.

After setting out the design steps, Jim Calloway's chapter brings the five steps together in a practical wrap-up chapter, with a focus on how design thinking can be used to improve your client service.

We then provide case studies that show how design thinking has been applied to solve particular challenges in the legal space. Our contributors are solo and small firm lawyers, big law attorneys, boutique firm founders, legal tech entrepreneurs, educators, and access to justice advocates.

The case studies provide a range of examples of where design thinking has been applied.

1. AJ Skogerson and Andrea McGinn share how design thinking propelled their firm, The Law Shop, forward in its efforts to make limited scope representation work for both clients and their firm.
2. Ginevra Saylor describes how she led a design thinking exercise within a large firm to reframe how the firm would work through litigation matters. She candidly reflects on the successes and limitations of the project, one which unfortunately was impacted by the COVID-19 pandemic.
3. Immigration law innovator Greg Siskind reflects on how he pioneered using the internet, and today continues to adapt more advanced technologies to provide helpful legal information and attract clients through direct-to-consumer online approaches. He considers how his approach focused on client needs and user experiences, which propelled his practice into online spaces well before many firms shifted to these areas.
4. Lisa Feldstein describes how she applied design thinking principles to solve an access to legal information challenge, which led to her developing online legal courses that help individuals and families and serves as an effective client pipeline.
5. Jordan M. Atin walks readers through how he built a legal software solution to enhance client experiences and reduce risks when drafting wills.

The diverse experiences and tips shared in these pages can be adapted to virtually any legal design challenge. The examples cut across different challenges and different solutions, but each share a core curiosity for the end-user experience as the driving force that leads to developing new ways of providing service.

Finally, the resources found at the end of this book should help you take the teachings and examples and work on your challenge equipped with tools to get results. The worksheet provides you with a canvas for your next legal design piece. And for those of you looking for more, our further readings provide additional resources.

Law is experiencing a renaissance period. It is rapidly shifting from a lawyer-centered to client-centered approach. Technology is being used to provide legal services in new and more affordable levels. Multidisciplinary approaches are fostering practice innovations. Even true solos are finding new ways to leverage people, processes such as design thinking, and technology to develop practices that give them meaning and their clients peace of mind.

We hope you can use this book to similarly help build your practice, and your legal community, wherever it may be. Wishing you success as you build the future of law.

PART I

Steps to Design Thinking

Now that we've convinced you that design thinking is not only approachable but also beneficial to you and your clients, let's get started! This section will introduce you to the five steps of the design thinking process, which are:

1. Empathize: Research Your Client's Needs
2. Define the Problem: A People-Centered Approach
3. Ideate: How to Solve the Problem
4. Prototype: Start to Create Solutions
5. Test and Refine: Try Your Solutions Out and Make Adjustments

Each chapter is written by a different author, and each author provides concrete, real-world examples of how they have used that step to improve a legal service, product, or process. As you read each chapter, reflect on whether you've also used that step before (perhaps unknowingly) to improve your firm, and how you might use it more often moving forward.

1

Step 1: Empathize: Research Your Clients' Needs

Jack Newton

For law firms in the digital age, simply "thinking like a lawyer" no longer suffices if you want to deliver high-quality legal services that meet the needs of modern clients. In this chapter, we'll discuss how to shift your mindset, learn more about your clients than you ever have before, and begin identifying key areas for improvement so you can stand out in an increasingly crowded and sophisticated legal market.

We'll cover a number of topics discussed in my book, *The Client-Centered Law Firm*, and other ways you can strengthen your firm's future by learning more from your clients. Topics we'll highlight include:

- Why the "lawyer-centered" model of legal service delivery is obsolete
- The importance of learning from other industries how to put your clients at the center of everything you do
- The value of routinely challenging your own assumptions, especially about your clients and their experiences with your firm
- How to build skills in empathy and deep listening so you can come to a deeper understanding of your clients

- Opening honest, two-way communication with your clients about what's working for them—and what isn't
- How to identify the various client "personas" who come to your firm, then map their specific client journeys from start to finish
- Identifying what you can learn from other firms, and applying those lessons to your firm
- Why you should never stop improving your firm's processes

Putting all these elements together, you'll see how researching your clients' needs and applying what you learn can have a tremendous positive impact on your firm, your clients, and your long-term success.

The first step is to reconsider the traditional "lawyer" mindset.

Stop Thinking Like a Lawyer

Throughout their educations and careers, lawyers are taught to think differently than those in other professions. When it comes to practicing law, this professional upbringing offers many advantages—but in terms of teaching people how to run law firms that address the needs of the modern legal market, this approach can have significant disadvantages as well. For example, thinking with a traditional "lawyer" mindset often blinds lawyers to important success factors, such as client preferences, business demands, market opportunities, and access and equity gaps.

So, what's the alternative to thinking like a lawyer? Thinking like a modern business owner.

To begin understanding your clients' needs in a new way, the first step is to take your "lawyer hat" off and put your "business owner hat" on. Now, many lawyers don't *like* thinking of themselves as business owners, but any lawyer with a partnership or ownership stake in a law firm *is* a business owner, and even associates and lawyers without equity stakes at larger firms can still benefit from embracing the business owner mentality. This is important because a law firm is, in fact, a business, and running one effectively means being aware of business concerns like market opportunities, efficiency, and—above all—the client experience.

Learning from other industries is particularly helpful because the legal industry hasn't been a shining example of innovation—so looking beyond the legal world shows you what top companies are doing to fuel their success. Companies like Amazon, Netflix, Uber, Airbnb, and others have realized that the best way to ensure their long-term growth is to gain a deep understanding of their customers and their markets—and to position their products and services accordingly.

If you're ready to stop thinking like a lawyer, you can start bringing lessons from the broader business world into your firm. And the No. 1 lesson the business world has to teach legal professionals is: Center everything you do around your clients.

Put Your Clients at the Center—of Everything

The predominant paradigm at most law firms continues to be what I refer to as the "lawyer-centered" model of legal service delivery. In this model, the lawyer sits at the center of everything the firm does, and everyone else—including the client—comes after.

What's needed, in order to take your firm where it needs to be in the years ahead, is to shift your practice's focus from *lawyer* centered to *client* centered. Prioritizing client-centered legal service delivery is better for you, your clients, and the future of your firm; we now live in a world where the customer experience is king, and law firms that understand this are attracting more clients, generating more positive reviews and referrals, and finding ways to expand access to more people who need legal services.

I speak often about the latent legal market, which is composed of all the would-be legal clients who aren't currently receiving legal assistance. According to a study conducted by the World Justice Project, 77 percent of legal problems in the United States don't receive any legal assistance,[1] which means that for every case a lawyer takes on, there are three other cases for which a lawyer didn't get hired. Unlocking the opportunity in this latent market is easily worth hundreds of billions of dollars per year, and the best way to realize this potential is to do things differently—by shifting away from the lawyer-centered model.

1. World Justice Project, Global Insights on Access to Justice (2018).

I should also note that by "client centered," I'm not saying "client *first*." You shouldn't let other areas of your practice and business suffer just to keep your clients happy—rather, you should be client *centered*, which means viewing your clients as the hub around which your entire firm revolves. Everything you do flows out of and back to your clients, creating a cohesive system where the clients' needs exist in harmony with the needs of the firm and its personnel.

Challenge Your Own Assumptions

One thing that is natural for many lawyers is to react to the concepts just mentioned by saying, "Well, maybe other lawyers and other firms don't know what they're doing, but I know *my* clients and I know how to run *my* law firm." And that may be true—you may know your clients well, and you may be great at running your firm—but you still likely could learn more. You might have an incomplete picture of your firm's own latent legal market (the people who aren't yet your clients, but could be), and you might be overlooking some opportunities for improved efficiency.

Take, for example, a study by the Clio research team, which looked at everyday consumers' overall satisfaction with legal services. Using a standardized assessment comparing legal to other industries, the results showed that, on average, legal services ranked fairly low—falling in line with the satisfaction rates for major airlines, banks, wireless carriers, and credit card companies.[2] The takeaway here is that the average law firm, successful or not, has room to improve.

To truly gain a complete picture of who needs your firm's services and how best to serve them, it's not enough to rely on gut feelings and preconceived ideas. Challenge your assumptions, throw out what you think you know, and start with a blank page. This will enable you to do the important work of learning from your clients, identifying any blind spots you may have, and really *knowing* what your clients want from your firm.

As alluded to earlier, doing this may also reveal new things you haven't thought about, including new slices of the legal market in your area that are just waiting for firms like yours to serve them.

2. Clio, Legal Trends Report (2018).

Practice Empathy

Starting with a blank page allows you to consider the legal client experience from a fresh vantage point. Now, let's talk about developing deep client empathy, one of the core values of a client-centered law firm.

To better understand your clients, you must first become better at empathizing with them. Simply put, the skill of practicing empathy is not taught well within the legal profession, neither in law schools nor in firms. On our *Matters* podcast on client-centered lawyering, renowned law professor and legal scholar Bill Henderson talks about how medical professionals and physicians are taught to be empathetic and hone their "bedside manner" throughout their training, but in legal, that's just not the case. Bill says many law firms have actually incentivized and rewarded practices that *don't* serve clients' best interests—often as a consequence of a lack of empathy.

Again, resist the urge to think, "I *do* empathize with my clients!" You very well may—and if so, you're ahead of the pack—but for the purposes of this discussion, I'm not solely talking about empathizing with your clients when you're on the phone or in a meeting with them. In this case, it's about considering what it's like for your clients and potential clients to work with you, as if you're seeing your firm through their eyes. In doing this, empathy can inform your entire client research process.

Client empathy is the force behind everything that will drive sustainable growth and success for your law firm. Deep client empathy helps you to understand what your clients experience when they interact with your firm, as well as what's going on in their lives. By using this empathetic practice, you can learn what your clients truly want and need from you, then take specific actions to change things at your firm and give your clients a more rewarding experience. This, in turn, will enhance your firm's reputation and business.

Give Your Clients the Floor

Here, we get into the real work of researching your clients' needs—and what better way to start than to actually ask your clients what they need?

Coming from a place of empathy, you'll want to begin opening up honest dialogues with your clients about their experiences with your firm—what works for them, what doesn't, and what things you can change in order to improve their experience. I know this seems simple, but many lawyers and firms don't do it. Instead, they just assume they know what their clients need, and they never take the time to go further than that.

Asking for feedback from your clients is a critical step to take toward becoming a client-centered law firm. Opening a forum for clients to speak candidly to you about your practice will enable you to see your firm through your clients' eyes, so you can understand deeply how best to serve them. Some simple ways to collect feedback are to actually ask clients about their experiences in one-on-one discussions, to host focus groups, or to conduct client surveys. There are lots of methods available to you—what matters is engaging your clients to glean whatever information will be most advantageous to your firm.

Identify Your Firm's Client Personas

Another key aspect of user or client research, not just in legal but in almost all areas of business, is to create customer "personas." In basic terms, a persona is a fictional character you create to represent what one of your customers might be like, so that you can "put a face" to one or more of your target audiences.

Identifying your target clients is valuable because it allows you to create strategies for more effectively reaching these clients, retaining them, and ensuring that they're happy with your services. Chances are, your clients don't all fit neatly into one uniform box; they might have different legal needs, come from different backgrounds, or have different expectations for client service. Breaking your target audiences into different groups gives you a chance to represent the diverse collection of people who turn to your practice for help.

Once you've broken your clientele into groups by their shared or differing characteristics, then you can build characters—a.k.a. personas—to represent each client (or potential client) group. This will help you visualize who they are as people and understand what they need from your firm. Crafting these personas will help you plan strategies, identify opportunities, and tailor your firm's processes to meet your clients' needs.

Create a Client Journey Map

Moving beyond the creation of personas, we get to one of my favorite techniques for becoming more client centered at your firm: client journey mapping.

Mapping your practice's client journey (or journeys) entails plotting out each stage of a client's experience with your law firm, from start to finish, so you can truly visualize what the entire process of working with your firm is like for the people you serve. It is a vital tool for the practice of challenging your own assumptions, as discussed earlier.

The legal client journey can generally be broken down into the following stages:

1. **Awareness:** When a potential client first realizes they have an issue that might be best solved through legal means
2. **Research:** When the potential client explores options to solve their legal issue, such as finding a lawyer
3. **Consultation:** When the potential client schedules an initial meeting with your firm to see if there's a good fit
4. **Decision:** When the potential client chooses your law firm, discusses payment, signs a retainer, and officially becomes your client
5. **During a Case:** When you work on the client's case or matter, until it is resolved
6. **Billing and Payment:** When you send the client an invoice for your services, and the client submits payment
7. **Review, Referral, Retention:** When the client provides a positive review, refers new clients to you, and decides to hire your firm again for future legal matters

Here's an example of how a client would move through these steps: Let's assume, for the purposes of this exercise, that you run a divorce and family law firm. A potential client named Sarah is going through the challenges of a divorce and arguing with her spouse about ownership of their property. Sarah initially begins realizing that she'll need the help of a lawyer (Awareness), so she starts looking for representation (Research), and she finds your firm's website. She schedules an appointment with you

(Consultation), after which she decides she'd like to hire your firm (Decision). Once she signs her retainer, you begin working on her divorce (During a Case), and eventually you and the lawyer for Sarah's spouse reach a settlement. You send Sarah her bill (Billing and Payment), and that's that—until two years later, when a couple of Sarah's friends go through divorces of their own, and she recommends your firm (Review, Referral, Retention). Later on, when Sarah has met someone new, they decide to sign a prenuptial agreement—and Sarah hires your firm again (Retention).

This is, by the way, an example of a *good* client journey. In many cases, Sarah's experience during a number of these stages could be frustrating and negative, perhaps because of poor communication from a law firm, an unsatisfactory settlement, or a surprisingly large bill. What this illustrates is that a positive client journey can create more reviews, referrals, and repeat customers—and a bad client journey will lead to lots of unsatisfied clients and damage to your firm's reputation.

To create an effective client journey map for your firm's clients, you'll need to consider how different cohorts of clients move through these stages during their engagements with your practice. Some useful ways to go about this include involving a cross-functional team of staff at your firm; referencing the client personas mentioned earlier to know which client journeys need the most attention; taking an inventory of all the potential interactions (a.k.a. touchpoints) from the start to the end of a client's experience with your firm; and interviewing your clients at different touchpoints throughout their journeys.

If you do client journey mapping right, it can shine a light on difference-making adjustments you can make to benefit both your clients and your firm.

Steal Like an Artist

There's a famous expression, "Good artists borrow, great artists steal." In other words, there's a tremendous advantage to be gained by looking at what others do well and emulating their success.

For your law firm, this means examining what other firms in your practice area across the country are doing. Are any of them innovating in particularly compelling ways? Are they experimenting with different models for billing or service delivery? How do they address some of the pain points and challenges that your firm customarily faces? If you see other firms doing something that seems like it could give your firm a competitive edge, it might be worth trying. Especially if that competitive edge improves the client experience you provide.

You can—and should—look at firms outside your practice area as well, not to mention other innovative companies in industries beyond legal. You don't need to invent everything from scratch yourself; you can turn to the most successful firms and companies in the world to identify powerful enhancements you can implement at your practice. If there are firms and organizations that inspire you with the work that they do or the services they provide, start asking yourself what makes these companies so great, what makes their customers so happy, and which things you can "steal" from them.

Try, and Try Again

This is old advice, yet it always bears repeating. Researching your clients' needs to make things better at your firm isn't something you do once and forget about—it's not a one-time thing. Quite the contrary, it's a process of continually checking in with your clients and ensuring that your firm is adapting to meet their needs, now and in the future.

In the technology industry, we call this process "iteration." At Clio, we iterate all the time by studying how we can make our products and features better for our customers, then devoting resources to make those changes. This is how tech companies keep up with their users' needs to provide the best customer experience possible—and it can be just as impactful as a practice for law firms.

One of my favorite theories is "the aggregation of marginal gains," popularized by James Clear, author of *Atomic Habits*. In it, Clear talks about how making a series of consistent, small improvements across everything you do will ultimately yield a huge positive change. If you improve every interaction your clients have with your law firm by even one percent, the aggregate client experience will be significantly better—and if you continuously strive to improve things by one percent, you will make enormous strides over time.

Together, the concepts of continuous iteration and the aggregation of marginal gains can be engines of change for your firm. Try them—and try them again.

Closing

I hope that the concepts discussed in this chapter will prove helpful to you as you begin researching your clients' needs in greater detail, and as you think about ways to create a better client experience at your firm.

Here's to a new age in legal service delivery—and the future of your firm.

Key Takeaways: Step 1

This is the first step in the design thinking process. The purpose of this step is to understand your clients' or users' needs in great detail so you design services and products that meet their needs.

- Stop thinking like a lawyer and start thinking more like a business owner.
- Put your clients at the center of everything you do.
- Challenge your own assumptions and examine your clients' experiences with fresh eyes.
- Practice deep empathy so you can see your clients in the full context of their lives.
- Give your clients the floor, soliciting direct feedback from them about your firm.
- Identify your firm's client personas, so you can put a face to different types of clients.
- Create client journey maps so you can scrutinize every interaction clients have with your firm, from the beginning to the end of their time with you.
- "Steal" great ideas from other law firms and nonlegal companies and use these ideas at your firm.
- Prioritize iteration—include it in your plan, budget for it, and make space to continuously improve. Keep making consistent, incremental improvements to your firm's practices and operations—over time, they'll add up.

2

Step 2: Define the Problem: A People-Centered Approach

Sarah McCoubrey and Meredith Brown

The Definition Stage: It Matters!

The second step in design thinking is defining the problem. The definition mode is a critical stage in your user-centered journey. In this stage, you expand on the evidence you gathered in the empathy stage and build a meaningful problem statement. Building your problem statement well is an essential element of user-centered design thinking. It is the foundation on which your solution will be built. In this chapter we set out a four-step process to bring the user into the process when defining the problem:

- Be humble
- Listen and learn
- Synthesize
- Test and refine

The problem statement is not merely a definition of the problem but sets out the challenge that you are solving for in a way that is *framed by your client* and is *actionable by you.*

Framed by your client—What does your client want and need from you? In order for you to solve the problem, you must clearly understand it. A client-centered, and human-centered approach, described in more detail later, ensures that you understand the problem from the perspective of the person who has the problem.

Actionable by you—How can you meet your client's need? In order for you to solve the problem, it must be articulated in a solvable way. This may mean breaking down a larger problem into smaller problem statements, ensuring that your problem scope is not too large, and it means ensuring that your problem statement generates responses.

Doing the definition stage well means:

- Setting aside sufficient time for this phase—don't shortchange the time spent defining the problem, because you want to get right to the solution!
- Gathering what you learned in your empathy stage and adding any missing data points
- Analyzing what your evidence tells you about the problem
- Synthesizing your evidence and analysis into a meaningful problem statement

Doing the definition stage well results in:

- An understanding of the problem from a people-centered perspective
- A problem statement that allows for idea generation
- A problem statement that has an actionable scope
- Time saved . . . if you don't get the problem statement right, you are doomed to repeat this phase!

Defining a "People-Centered" Legal Problem

Legal professionals group legal problems into substantive categories—property, family, criminal, immigration. But legal problems are actually life problems and people do not think of their legal issues in these substantive categories. Instead, their life problems are intertwined with complex relationships, histories, and implications beyond the legal ones. A case may present you with an intellectual or a strategic challenge. Meanwhile the client may be losing sleep, manifesting health problems, jeopardizing their employment or eroding their relationships. Legal issues can be scary and destabilizing.

Designing legal services to really meet people's needs, to really put them at the center of their legal issues, requires that you not just recognize how the issue affects someone's whole life but also recognize that their priorities or goals may not be the same as yours. Lawyers often measure legal success in monetary awards and judicial pronouncements. People might define success differently—do they or their children still have strong relationships with their extended family? Have they had to go looking for a new job? Were they able to participate in key family events? Did they have to move? Did they deplete their savings? Did it cost them their privacy? What have they lost during the legal process? Putting people at the center of their legal problems means listening to the intangible costs or goals that they prioritize.

Working from a people-centered perspective is also good for business. For too long lawyers have disenfranchised people from their legal issues. Only those who have the finances, education, literacy, and social capital to work with a lawyer have historically relied on legal services. Understanding life problems from a user perspective offers the opportunity to identify whole new ways to provide legal services and meet people's needs who haven't been well served by conventional legal services. When rethinking how you deliver legal services, it is critical to not limit the possibilities by only considering the needs of your current clients. Not only can you build a people-centered practice, but you can also fundamentally shift, and grow, your client base by designing your legal services to meet more people's legal needs.

By defining your problem statement based on an understanding of the goals and needs of people immersed in their life problems—not the sanitized versions that can emerge after legal analysis and argument—you will open your design process to this broader market, meeting real, unmet needs.

Language

As you start the process of articulating the problem statement you are designing around, the language you use can make a big difference. Working from the experiences of your existing clients might limit your possibilities to those of people who are already using legal services. Are you only thinking about your clients? Are you thinking about people as *users* of the legal system? Customers? Rights holders? Expanding your thinking, and your language, to include a broader picture of the people facing legal problems expands the scope of your problem statement.

Think Big

For too long lawyers have made only small adjustments to how we interact with our clients, driven by changes in technology or the law. We have not seen the fundamental rethink that has transformed so many other sectors, from health care to airline travel to banking. Being ready to learn and redesign legal practice is an opportunity to bring your own creativity and entrepreneurial ideas to the business of law. As outlined in Step 1, this is a process of making people the hub of your business model.

The lawyer-client paradigm brings assumptions about who is in charge and who holds the solutions. Thinking about people navigating legal dimensions of their life as users of the legal system and our services as tools to meet their goals transforms that power dynamic. Clients can articulate their own priorities and decide when and how to rely on the justice system. Perhaps if more services were designed with this broad appreciation of user needs, more people would seek out legal help, believing it would truly meet their needs.

Recognizing whose problem you are trying to solve is critical to this rethink. You must do more than consider the client, the court system, the firm, or even your own experience as a lawyer. Instead, start by understanding and then responding to people's unmet legal needs.

This is a fundamental shift from typical marketing, or service improvements, to using design thinking to reengineer legal practice to be truly people centered.

Steps to Defining the Problem

Step One: Be Humble

Your legal knowledge is a tool, but it does not give you complete insight into people's lives. This isn't a process of making your firm work better, it is a process of meeting real needs, as people define them for themselves.

Don't start with someone's experience of the firm, or of legal services, but start by considering how people experience legal problems. Recognize that your assumptions and your own experience are not theirs. The problems are not yours and you will not be the one to live with the results. Meeting people's legal needs cannot be about the experience of the lawyer.

Your Step One Action
Check your biases: Before you sit with your client, intentionally set aside 2 minutes to think about your own mindset. What are you bringing to the discussion? Do you have pre-set beliefs or expectations that will prevent you from really hearing what the client is saying? Are you already focused on the part of their problem you find interesting? Have you already 'solved' the client's problems in your mind? What assumptions are you making about success? What constitutes success for the client? Call out your own biases and set them aside so that you are truly ready to meet the client where they are, not where you are or think they should be.

Step Two: Listen and Learn

As lawyers, we are already experienced in asking questions and gathering information to make our case or solve a client's legal problem. As innovators, we can build on that skill set and move from asking questions to fit our client into the preexisting legal model to asking people-centered questions that really dig into the WHY of the problem.

Listening is an intentional act. In order to really understand the problem, you must actively listen to the client, gather the data they are giving you, and ask questions that will allow you to really learn from what you are hearing.

You began the process of listening in the empathy stage. Now is the time for you to refine that listening and to learn from it.

Your Step Two Action
"The Five Whys": The Five Whys method was originally developed by Sakichi Toyoda as a part of the process of evolving Toyota's manufacturing processes. The process involves taking the initial statement of the problem and asking why repeatedly until the "true" problem emerges. This is not you parroting the word "why" but rather taking your client's first statement and asking a specific *why* question about it.

Use this method to move from the first statement of the problem—how the client is experiencing the issue—toward the root cause of the issue. There is no perfect number of times to ask *Why*—you may get to your insight with three whys or with seven. Sometimes, your line of questioning will reveal multiple root causes, requiring different lines of asking Why and evolving problem statements.

Here is a sample of how the Five Whys process could be used to dig for the root cause of a problem:

The problem is first given as: The client does not want to pay the bill.

1. Why don't they want to pay? They feel the bill is too high.
2. Why do they feel the bill is too high? They do not think the firm did as much work as it charged.
3. Why do they think the firm did not do the work? They do not understand or see what the firm did to earn the money.
4. Why don't they understand what the firm did? They were not given a clear explanation of the firm's work.
5. Why were they not given a clear explanation? The firm's process does not include time spent with the client or a document that accompanies the bill to explain the work and how the value of the work will be calculated.

If you had not conducted this Five Whys exercise, you may have assumed that the client was trying to avoid paying you. You may have missed the insight that your firm was failing to provide an important service to the clients, perpetuating the problem.

Step Three: Synthesize

Now that you have gathered data about the problem from the client's perspective and you have dug into the root causes and gleaned insight, it is time to distill this to the problem statement that will guide your ideation and solution.

A Spectacular Point of View

Preserves emotion and the individual you're designing for.
Includes strong language.

Uses sensical wording.
Includes a strong insight.
Generates lots of possibilities.
[Design thinking bootleg, d.school at Stanford University, https://dschool.stanford.edu/resources/design-thinking-bootleg]

Your problem statement should be given from the point of view of the user (your client, the group of people with the problem, etc.), should articulate the need or the issue, and explain the insight/root cause that you have gleaned.

Remember that you are trying to define the problem in a way that will generate solution possibilities so consider the scope of the problem, use compelling language, and keep the focus on your clients.

Using the example from the preceding Five Whys exercise, here is a sample problem statement resulting from that exercise.

> *Problem statement: People who hire our firm (description of the user) think we are overcharging them (the issue/need of the client) because we are not providing them with enough information to understand the work that we are doing on their behalf and its value (the root cause/compelling insight).*

Your Step Three Action

Using the data and the insights you have gained through active listening and inquiry, build your problem statement using this template:

> [Person/people who are the center of the problem in a descriptive way]. . .needs [use a verb]. . .because [your compelling insight].

Step 4: Test and Refine

Once you have a problem statement, the next step is to test it, and be ready to edit and refine it. This is the first of many iterative steps in the design process where your thinking adapts to new information and multiple perspectives. For some design thinking efforts, there are real people you can test your problem statement with. Share the statement and listen to them explain if they agree or would modify the statement.

Often, when rethinking services, it is awkward to ask potential users of your services to help you improve (though eventually, it is useful to test your ideas with real people). For now, you can start to test the statement against *personas* of different users to see how different clients will see your legal services differently and may respond differently to your innovations. Personas are a technique in design thinking to understand and test your innovations. This means going further than thinking about your clients as personas to imagining how people experience legal problems, building a persona based on what you hear about legal needs and then testing your innovation's relevance for these personas.

Your Step Four Action

Articulate four or five personas of clients you want to serve. Be creative—give them names, ages. Imagine who lives in their houses, what kind of work they do. Where do they go on holiday? What makes them happy or anxious? You can draw on attributes of different people you have worked with and different people you have interacted with outside of the lawyer-client relationship.

Once you have written out your personas, consider your problem statement from the perspective of each persona—does it ring true? Would they add something to the statement? Refine your problem statement based on this persona testing.

Applying this approach to our sample, let's consider our problem statement against some personas:

> *Problem statement: People who hire our firm think we are over-charging them because we are not providing them with enough information to understand the work that we are doing on their behalf and its value.*
>
> Persona 1: Adil is a 38-year-old, single parent and small business owner. He takes his kids hiking when he can, going offline as much as possible. He loves a challenge but is worried about long-term stability for his family. Adil is growing his business and is always busy, responding with quick replies by text or email. He is having his employment contracts reviewed by the firm.

Persona 2: Ede is a 58-year-old teacher, getting ready to retire. She loves to kayak and garden and dreams of a trip to Italy. She has a pretty good understanding of complex relationships and human dynamics but gets flustered easily when someone corrects her. She is appealing a benefits decision made by the insurer after she was hurt in a car accident.

Persona 3: Markus is a 24-year-old new immigrant enrolled in a technical program at the local college. He is always nervous that he has missed the point of a comment, even though his literacy and understanding are very good. An uncle has died recently and he is the nearest family member so he is trying to handle the estate and paperwork.

Testing the Problem Statement:

Persona	Motivation	Needs	Emotions	Attributes	Possible reaction to getting a bill	Changes to problem statement
Adil	Trying to save money	Quick, simple communi-cation	Impatient	Inattentive Ambitious	Skims for the total amount; prone to miss the amount	Too much detail
Ede	Tired of working and being taken advantage of	Confidence and respect	Optimistic Insecure	Trusting	Gets lost in the list of tasks and disburse-ments; quick to think the amount is too high	Too over-whelming
Markus	Worried about pro-tocols and rules	Clear under-standing	Fearful—Doesn't want to make any mistakes; Grief	Sensitive Dutiful	Isn't familiar with legal terms and is embarrassed to ask for clarification	Unclear language

Having considered these personas' reactions to your problem statement, it is clear that this issue is not just whether the firm bill includes enough information, but also whether it is presented in a way that different readers can understand and process. Based on this testing against your personas, you might revise your problem statement:

> *REVISED problem statement: People who hire our firm think we are overcharging them because we are not providing them with enough information IN A FORMAT THEY UNDERSTAND, about the work that we are doing on their behalf and its value.*

This simple example is a template for how the testing process, whether against real people's reactions or persona reactions, is a tool to strengthen your problem statement before you start to design solutions.

Be Trauma Informed

When you are engaging in any relationship with individuals, it is important to bring a trauma-informed lens to your relationship. This is particularly true when talking with clients about their legal issues and experiences. Legal conflict often involves traumatic events, or emerges from people's reactions, developed because of trauma in their lives.

Being trauma informed means that you are aware of the impact of trauma on the brain and the body and that you actively implement strategies to avoid exacerbating trauma-related problems. It also means listening differently and recognizing how a client's experiences of trauma may lead to reactions or priorities different from your own. Their articulation of the problem, and the solution, may be different.

A trauma-informed practice is important to building trust with clients and to helping those clients navigate the legal issues they are experiencing. Failure to be trauma-informed may result in harm to your clients and in your inability to provide meaningful legal services to them.

As you are innovating your practice, consider how well you and your colleagues are practicing a trauma-informed practice. Learn what you can do to enhance your skills. As you grow your understanding and your approach, greater opportunities to ideate and innovate in the service of your clients will present themselves.

Trauma-Informed Legal Practice Resources

ABA Commission on Lawyer Assistance Programs. *Compassion Fatigue*. n.d. https://www.americanbar.org/groups/lawyer_assistance/resources/compassion_fatigue.

GPSolo. "Compassion Fatigue: An Interview with Judge Jeremy Fogel." *GPSolo Magazine* June 2019. https://www.americanbar.org/groups/gpsolo/publications/gp_solo/2019/may-june/compassion-fatigue.

Rebecca Howlett and Cynthia Sharp. "The Legal Burnout Solution: How Secondary Trauma Impacts the Mental Health of Legal Professionals." June 2021. https://www.americanbar.org/content/aba-cms-dotorg/en/groups/gpsolo/publications/gpsolo_ereport/2021/june-2021/legal-burnout-solution-how-secondary-trauma-impacts-mental-health-legal-professionals.

Solving the Problem

Now that you have a problem statement, based on a genuine process of listening and learning, you are ready to start finding and experimenting with responses or solutions to the problem. As you do this, you may stumble on new insights that necessitate further refining of the problem statement. Your personas can make appearances at different stages of your design process, letting you test different ideas in the same way that you tested the problem statement.

Designing legal services, based on this clearly articulated, well-grounded problem statement sets you up to make meaningful, relevant changes to your service model to meet real needs without relying on your own assumptions or limiting yourself to your current client base. You are ready to move on to step three: ideate.

Key Takeaways: Step 2

This is the second step in the design thinking process. The purpose of this step is to define the problem you are trying to solve from your clients' perspective with enough specificity to start brainstorming ideas in Step 3.

- The problem statement is not merely a definition of the problem but sets out the challenge that you are solving for in a way that is framed by your client and is actionable by you.
- The problem statement should not be based on substantive legal categories and your goals and needs, but should instead be based on what your client is experiencing, the legal issue, and their goals and needs.
- Create a problem statement that will work for clients you currently serve and potential clients who you don't currently serve but aim to.
- Use this four-step process for defining the problem:

1. Humility. Be humble, check your biases.
2. Listen and learn. Ask why repeatedly until the "true" problem emerges.
3. Synthesize. Use the data and the insights you have gathered through listening and inquiry and build your problem statement using this template: [Person/people who are the center of the problem in a descriptive way]. . .needs [use a verb]. . .because [your compelling insight].
4. Test and refine. Articulate four or five client personas, consider your problem statement from the perspective of each persona, and adjust/refine the problem statement as needed.

3

Step 3: Ideate: How to Solve the Problem

Lori Gonzalez

Step 3 of design thinking is ideation. This step is the most creative of the five stages and requires us to intentionally unleash creativity and brainstorm solutions without boundaries or a need for quality and excellence. As we move into discussions of the ideation phase of design thinking, suspending the need to come up with the correct, most perfect, or "right" answer to the problem statement is crucial to a successful outcome. Ideation is best served when limiting beliefs are suspended and an attitude of anything goes is embraced. The clients' needs have been identified and clearly stated—now is the time to produce a wild and radical list of solutions. As ideas are created, shared, and brought forward, all ideas should be welcomed. Resist the urge to immediately throw out or dismiss bad ideas. For the ideation phase, there are no bad ideas, and anyone involved in this stage should feel comfortable proposing even the most preposterous notions. Remembering to empathize with the stakeholders you invite to the ideation phase is just as necessary to ensure success as it was in researching your clients' needs. Creating a safe, open, and approachable environment for all invited is required to ensure a successful ideation phase.

Go Beyond the Lawyer Mindset

Innovation requires many traits that are not natural strengths among professionals trained in law. In his "Herding Cats: The Lawyer Personality Revealed" Dr. Larry Richard identified six traits that lawyers tend to score either abnormally high or low in compared to the general public.[1] Those six traits were:

- A higher than average level of skepticism
- A higher than average level of urgency
- A higher than average level of autonomy
- A lower than average level of resilience
- A lower than average level of sociability

These personality traits allow lawyers to flourish in the practice of law, but true creativity is unleashed, and real innovation happens when:

- Skepticism is suspended
- Patience is a natural part of the process and time constraints are suspended or minimized
- Teamwork is encouraged, celebrated, and fostered
- Failure is allowed, required, and celebrated
- Experimentation, communication, and interactions with a broad range of individuals is regular and constant

Therefore, especially in the ideation phase, a multidisciplinary approach with individuals of varying skill sets and true inclusion is required. All members of a firm should be a part of the ideation process. Also, consider inviting others outside of the team such as technology professionals, business development professionals, law students, and even clients. Office managers, billing clerks, secretaries, and interns are also great additions. Ensuring that a wide range of skills, personalities, and strengths are at the table will maximize creativity and produce a variety of solutions.

1. Larry Richard, Herding Cats: The Lawyer Personality Revealed, lawyerbrain.com.

Think Outside the Conference Room

Another useful way to spur creativity and bring forth a larger quantity of solutions is to rethink the space where brainstorming happens. If others are invited to a space that is typically controlled by management/lawyers, it could create unintentional boundaries and counter the team-like approach needed in this step. A comfortable location is very useful, perhaps with sofas and sitting chairs versus the typical conference room table. Many large companies will rent "innovation hubs" in co-working or e-space events to help spur creative thinking. Embrace large and open spaces and provide snacks for participants. Whiteboards, blank walls, Post-it notes (lots and lots), and colorful markers are also useful tools for this step. For those meeting virtually, look at mind-mapping tools and creative white-board/note-taking tools to ensure no ideas are lost.

Embrace "No Bad Ideas"

After the team has been assembled, be sure to fully explain the problem statement as defined in step 2. The solution that will ultimately be selected needs to be technically feasible (a functional product or an effective service), economically viable (affordable and realistic to implement), and desirable for the user (meets the real human need.) Stress to the team that this part of the process is where there are no rules, no limitations, and no bad ideas. All ideas should be freely welcomed, celebrated, and considered.

A favorite way to inspire idea creation is the timed Post-it note approach. Provide every team member a set of Post-it notes and a window of time when all ideas should be placed on individual Post-it notes. Make sure the problem statement is displayed where each team member can easily be reminded. A three-minute window can be an effective timeframe, especially when team members are new to this process. Guidance to provide the team includes:

1. There is no minimum or maximum number of ideas.
2. Ideas do not need to be vetted, simply written down, regardless of the feasibility.

3. Individuals should work alone, and ideas do not need to be discussed as a team.
4. Each idea is written on a separate Post-it note and all notes are collected at the end of the three minutes.

Once the three minutes are up, the ideas should be briefly explained or discussed as a team. This is not where a prototype is built (more on this stage in the next chapter), but instead just brief clarification is established as needed for the team to understand the basics of each idea. No ideas should be dismissed or debated, just clarified if needed. Once all clarifications are provided, move the Post-it notes to an area where each one can be fully displayed. Each team member is then provided a limited number of "votes." These votes can be stickers or written dots on a Post-it note. Get creative, if possible, but votes should not be easily identified back to the individual, as voting is simply to aggregate the interest in any one idea. There are no rules to how these votes are used—votes can be spread out among several ideas, or all the votes can be placed on a single idea. Dispel the idea of "fairness" and allow each member to decide how intensely they feel about ideas using their votes—even if it is one of their own ideas.

Listen to Diverse Perspectives

Once all votes are placed, tally the top ideas, and discuss them in detail as a group. It is not necessary to build the idea into a working model, but instead the goal should be to decide as a group what idea (or small set of ideas) are ready to move into the prototyping stage. While this process can be fun, engaging, and hopefully a great team-building experience, it can also be difficult to suspend the typical skepticism of the legal field. Be sure the entire team is empathizing with each other, keeping the clients' needs in mind, and actively listening. This can be difficult for legal professionals and especially lawyers, who are much more autonomous and used to a more competitive versus collaborative environment.

Even the most experienced at design thinking can easily forget the true benefits of an entire team's experiences and ideas. My team handles a large volume of data entry. Our clients needed us to continue to improve our efficiency so that we could produce records faster and with fewer data entry errors. After researching various ways to improve a group's efficiency and accuracy, a decision was made to limit the hours worked by each team member. Deciding how to implement the reduced hours was something to be workshopped as a team. As the CEO and individual who had the most experience and research knowledge regarding this type of improvement, I had made several assumptions that needed to be challenged. After having an afternoon of food and fellowship, the team began the ideation phase of how to improve efficiency by reducing hours. To my surprise, a team member suggested a six-hour workday, five days a week. As we moved through the voting phase, it was clear that this schedule was preferred by the entire team. I had mistakenly assumed the team would prefer a four-day workweek, which would have been harder to manage for our clients' sake.

Implementing this new schedule was a breeze, because the team had real ownership in the entire process. There was very little change management required because the idea originated from the team. And allowing the team to build the process (prototype) also ensured that any potential needs were addressed by the team as a whole and everyone worked for the best outcome for all. Ultimately, our reduced schedule—which was ten hours less of data entry a week per person—resulted in more data entry with fewer errors. As we discussed the six-hour idea, it was discovered that the last two hours of the day were filled with distractions because of burnout. Reducing the hours meant the team gave their best for six hours, then clocked out, making happier team members each day.

Obviously, this exercise also shows how even service-based processes can be improved upon with design thinking. Going back to Chapter 1 where we discussed the billing process, how might a receptionist who understands how payments are taken improve the billing process? Or the office manager/billing clerk who understands how often billing entries/fees are effectively cut? But what happens when we move a step further into solving unmet legal needs. After those needs have been identified and researched, what could a diverse team of individuals create as a new service? Ensuring diversity (such as, for example, age, ethnicity, position, education, skill set, sexual orientation, and gender identity) allows for a true creative approach to the complexity of what your users need and will result in the best ideas possible.

Summing Up

Design thinking is a process concerned with solving complex problems. It is a process developed by designers in a highly consumer-centric world. The core of it puts human beings first at every stage. As you work through the ideation phase, remember this stage is often one of the most fun and engaging. Be sure you build the process to fully embrace and empathize with those who will work with you to create ideas. And most of all. . .remember to have fun!

Key Takeaways: Step 3

Ideation is the third step in the design thinking process. The purpose of this step is to brainstorm as many ideas as possible without restraint or judgment so that you can create the best solution to the problem you defined in Step 2.

- Ideation, the most creative of the five design thinking stages, works best when judgment and limiting beliefs are suspended and an anything goes approach is allowed.
- Innovation requires many traits that are not natural strengths of lawyers; therefore, a multidisciplinary approach with individuals of varying skill sets is required.
- Consider holding your brainstorming session in a comfortable space that inspires creativity and promotes idea sharing (i.e., not the usual conference room!).
- Utilize the diversity of your team to evaluate and expand the ideas once vetted.

4

Step 4: Prototype: Start to Create Solutions

Hersh Perlis and Chris Bentley

Introduction

Prototyping generally comes at the fourth step in the design thinking process. This is where you pull together what you have learned from your research, and from exercises such as the user persona, problem identification, and ideation, and start to create something tangible, such as a model for a new legal product, a new or improved legal service, or an improved process.

While a prototype is often thought of as a thing, *prototyping* is as much an approach. It involves "creating" something, but its core value is in why you are doing it, what you find out from others (and your own reflections), and what you do as a result of that information. As we will see, there is rarely one "build" of a prototype. Each revision builds on insights and data learned from the previous versions, forming a continuous loop of improvements and iterations.

We want to emphasize that you can, and should, use design thinking to improve a process. It follows that a prototype can be a new or improved process. The language of prototyping often suggests that it is a thing, but it can involve the addition or elimination of steps in a process, or an entirely new process itself. Indeed, modernizing elements of our justice system requires the "rethinking" that is at the heart of design thinking, and for the purpose of this chapter, prototyping. The entity that you create is the new process.

In this chapter, we will explore the basics of what prototyping is, the purpose of creating a prototype, the means of doing so, and the benefits you receive from taking the time and energy to get the most out of this stage of design thinking. Like design thinking itself, prototyping is as much of a process with a purpose as it is a thing. We will use the experiences from some of the Legal Innovation Zone startups that we've worked with and other entrepreneurs as case studies to help you understand the benefits and the pitfalls of not following a process. Our hope is that this chapter will help bring some clarity and demystify one of the most essential steps in the design thinking approach—prototyping.

What?

What is prototyping? The Interaction Design Foundation defines a prototype as "a simple experimental model of a proposed solution used to test or validate ideas, design assumptions and other aspects of its conceptualisation quickly and cheaply."[1] A prototype helps you tell a story and receive feedback/input in a fast, meaningful, and cost-effective way.

Margaret Hagan, head of the Design School at Stanford, describes different stages of prototyping. The earliest stages are extensions of your ideas or brainstorming sessions. They help you distill or reduce an idea to its essence.[2] This suggests that the prototyping stage begins quite early and underlines the fact that the stages of design thinking are not as defined as the labels suggest.

1. https://www.interaction-design.org/literature/article/design-thinking-get-started-with-prototyping.
2. https://lawbydesign.co.

The "prototype" itself can come in a range of forms. It could be a drawing, client journey map, model, or even a robot, an early-stage product or advanced technology solution. Prototyping can be as simple as pictures on a piece of paper or images on a computer screen, or as complex as a digital product that is almost ready to be sold and used. The type of prototype you build will depend on your "why" of prototyping.

Why?

A prototype is created for a purpose. The type and complexity of the prototype normally depends on what stage of development you are at, and what the purpose was of building the prototype. By purpose we don't mean the ultimate goal; rather, what do you hope to achieve by building the prototype. This is the "why" of prototyping.

Benefits of Prototyping

Andrew Arruda, co-founder of Ross Intelligence and current co-founder and CEO at Automate Medical,[3] captures the benefits of prototyping by stating that "prototyping is like doing your homework, why would you leave anything to chance?" Launching a new product or service is challenging, but the more effort you invest at the front end, the more you are able to remove risk from the venture. If, by the time you release a new service or product, you have already shared and spoken to tens or hundreds of potential users and/or paying customers who have used your prototype and provided feedback, there should be few surprises when you ultimately launch. You will know whether there is value in your solution, and what that value is.

How?

So how do you go about this? Essentially, you match the stage of the solution development with the sophistication of the prototype.

---

3. Automate Medical makes it easy for startups to build in health by building open-source development tools for health data standards. https://www.automatemedical.com.

Early-stage prototyping forces you to focus your thoughts on a key problem and idea. It requires an articulation of a problem/solution path. What is the problem you are trying to solve? Who are you solving it for? What is your solution? How do you move from problem to solution? The path needs to be clear, and logical, or success is unlikely to follow.

As you proceed, you will get feedback from others. The prototype develops in form and sophistication based on feedback, and the further development encourages additional useful input.

The most common types of prototypes are drawings, wireframes, and coded minimum viable products. Before we describe each of them and discuss when they are usually used, there are two important points to remember. First, always keep your focus on the problem and, second, make sure you have deep knowledge, or are able to gain deep knowledge, around the process you are solving for.

Keeping your focus on the problem will ensure that all of your energy and resources are kept aligned on solving the problem for the user. Think of your problem as your North Star. As you share your idea and prototype with more and more potential users/customers you will start to receive a substantial amount of feedback. Assessing the feedback against the problem will help you separate the relevant from the noise and the useful from the merely interesting.

You need a deep understanding of the process that the product or service will work in. Knowing your customers' payment structures, workflow, corporate structure, or technology capabilities, for example, will help ensure your innovation fits within your customers' needs and operations. The best products and service offerings can easily be left unused simply because the innovator didn't understand something simple, such as how customers were being charged for a service, or which core research, data, or customer relationship management technology was being used.

The early research and exploration of both the problem and the process is sometimes rushed, but it should not be. It is an investment worth making. In the innovation world you often hear of sprints, but this is not a time to sprint. The extra exploration time at the front end will improve the chances of success, and reduce the likelihood of painful mistakes, later on.

Technology or process? Both. First, you are developing a better solution for a problem, not a piece of technology for its own sake. Focus on the problem first and always. Second, too much of the innovation discussion in law focuses on an app or other piece of technology as the route to a more modern approach to service delivery, and then equates that with a solution to your problem. It might be, but that depends on the problem you are solving for.

The solution might be found in new technology, in a combination of technology and a new process, or predominantly in a new process where technology plays little part other than facilitating an entirely new approach. You need to understand the process, and the consumer journey through that process, to begin to understand whether the solution might work. You then need to build a prototype that you can test with consumers, obtain feedback on it, and then refine and improve it.

Drawing

A picture is worth a thousand words. Drawing is often the first type of prototyping used in the early stages of the innovation journey. These drawings can be one page filled with stick-people and other simple objects, or a page with eight squares where each square is a step in the journey. They could also be several pages showing a step-by-step process or journey the user will go through while using the service, and they could also show the mindset they are in just prior to or after the service. Do not be intimidated if you are not an artist, as most of us are not. The pictures are there to help you focus and visualize.[4]

Drawings are ideally suited to both help focus your ideas and as a means to encourage early feedback on an idea or possible new additions to a product. Patrick Hartford, founder of NoticeConnect,[5] keeps a notebook next to his computer. When he gets an idea, he draws it to help him visualize the concept. Drawing has two key benefits for Patrick. First, it helps him bring his thoughts together in a rational way. Crystallizing ideas in a sketch,

---

4. Here is a link to one of our favorite user journey maps created by Erin Balderson showing the "First Uber Ride Experience" http://www.erinbalderson.com/uber-journey-map.

5. Ontario lawyer Patrick Hartford founded NoticeConnect in 2015 as a better way for executors to advertise for creditors. Since then the company has grown into a broader information solution for will and estates professionals, integrated with practice-specific software. https://www.noticeconnect.com.

however simple, can help you see the strengths and weaknesses, decide if the idea is worth pursuing, and make any appropriate adjustments.

The second purpose of drawing the idea is for storytelling and sharing with others. Patrick has found over the years that it is much easier and more productive if he has a visual representation of a potential new product or offering. He is convinced that he has saved hundreds of hours of back and forth with his developers and potential customers because of the clarity his drawings have provided. Being able to visualize a journey or see the impact and possibilities of a new product or service can help ensure that the feedback you receive from a potential client, customer, or developer is more relevant and meaningful than just a simple conversation.

Wireframes

Wireframes are another form of prototyping and are most often used when your idea includes a technology solution. No coding experience or deep technology knowledge is required. They can often be created for free or quite affordably using online tools such as Figma, Sketch, Adobe XD, or Miro. Like drawings, building a wireframe is a simple and quick way to both show a potential customer how your new product will operate and as a means to encourage feedback on new processes or offerings you are planning to build.

Wireframes are literally just images of what your product will look like and how it will operate.[6] There is no "coding" behind the images. The wireframe consists of a series of screen shots, with one to three clickable buttons, that can take your customer on a journey through your product.

The goal is to give potential customers an opportunity to get a sense of the user experience, and see how the product or service flows from beginning to result. The speed and simplicity of building a wireframe mean that it is efficient and affordable to continuously iterate/adjust as you observe how people are using it and even where they are clicking. This information and data will be priceless as you start to put real dollars and energy into a working prototype.

---

6. Here is a link with more information on wireframing and a good image illustrating what a wireframe can look like. https://blog.prototypr.io/why-you-shouldnt-skip-your-wireframing-1f7a70d5c125.

Building a Working Prototype—MVP (Minimally Viable Product)

Once you have accumulated feedback, learned from it, and made the necessary adjustments, it is time to build the more operational prototype, called the minimally viable product (MVP). This is not necessarily what the final product will be built from, and it will not have all the bells and whistles of a polished final product. The goal here is to build something that can perform the main operations you have been telling your customers about.

There are two distinct paths to building this prototype. One involves using one or more off-the-shelf technology products, which would enable you to give your potential customers a good idea of what you are building, while the other uses coding and building a product from scratch. In either situation, this is the point where you will want to find a technology lead or a technology advisor to help drive the process.

Whether you are a lawyer looking to enhance your practice or a legal tech entrepreneur, there are two main advantages to building an MVP with off-the-shelf products: time and speed. Using readily available products will drastically reduce the time it takes for you to build the MVP and generally comes with more certainty and affordability around costs. For example, for legal product development, you could use an app builder or automation tool such as Fliplet or Typeform. This is often a short-term solution to your final build, but it will allow you to get something in the hands of your potential customers quickly and efficiently.

Off-the-shelf products have many benefits, but also some challenges. They are generally less flexible to specific changes you may need down the road, often come with terms that may tie you to the product for longer than you would like, and generally are not as easy to scale with as you grow your product or service offerings. However, the speed and price often make this the best first step for many entrepreneurs.

Building a new product from scratch is often the route people jump to in order to build their MVP. The benefit is that you can build something to your specific design needs with the options and offerings you envisioned for your product. You are not limited to one type of technology or option as you change your product offering. However, unless you are an experienced developer, this is going to mean that you either bring on a developer/chief technology officer or outsource the build to a development firm.

Outsourcing can bring certainty around costs and timing, and lowers the risk of not getting a working prototype. The challenges are that each additional change, or iteration, which is at the heart of prototyping, will add time and money to the product build. Think of changes you make to a renovation plan. Partnering or bringing on a developer means you have better day-to-day oversight; however, you will need to make sure you know how to hire or partner with the right person who has the skills you are looking for.

Building a product yourself based on existing products has many uncertainties, but it often will pay dividends later in the process when you end up with a product specifically built for your customers' needs.

There is no right or wrong path to take. It very much depends on your needs, abilities, and resources. *As always, speaking to others who have gone through similar journeys is highly recommended.* Complexity can often kill a great idea. It is important at every stage, but especially in the early build, to remember to focus on the problem you are solving and leave all the other "nice to haves" for a later time.

Feedback

"If you build it they will come" made for a great movie line but it certainly could not be further from the truth when it comes to building a product or creating a new service people will use. The reason we start with pictures, then move to wireframes, and only then to the more expensive coded prototypes is so we can more easily and effectively adjust to feedback. Early prototyping is relatively easy and inexpensive, and can be adjusted easily to the customers' needs. The later prototyping is more involved, takes longer, and is more expensive. By that time you should have the confidence that customers will be both interested in the product and willing to pay for it.

Repeat entrepreneur Mona Datt, founder of several companies, including Loom Analytics[7] and eDecree, speaks often about her past experience of skipping over parts of the earlier prototyping stages and going right to building the "perfect" product. Mona had a great idea and knew custom-

7. Loom Analytics uses data analytics to empower legal and insurance operations teams to turn their business processes into connected digital workflows. https://www.loomanalytics.com.

ers were in need of a certain type of product, however she didn't share what she was building along the way. When Mona finally came out with her product, after spending significant sums of money on developers, the customers did not line up to pay. The product was good and solved a problem they all were experiencing. However, the absence of ongoing customer feedback and insight resulted in her missing key customer expectations about the user experience and how it needed to interact with their current processes. Mona learned from that experience, and now when she is building new products, potential customers have input on a weekly basis as they go through the different iterations of a build. This helps ensure that when the prototype is ready to use it fits properly into the current workflow of her potential customers.

Sometimes, the feedback you receive leads to a clarity in thinking. That clarity might be rather challenging in its result. This is what Derek and Shane faced early on as they co-founded Law Scout, which turned into Founded. The company they helped co-found, Law Scout, was developed to help entrepreneurs and small business owners connect with lawyers for fixed-fee rates to set up their companies and obtain a range of legal services for early-stage ventures. It did not take long for them to realize that however good their product and process was, it was not going to be able to scale to the point where a meaningful number of people were prepared to pay for it in its current form for the endeavor to be viable/profitable. This was the ultimate feedback.

They learned. They pivoted. Their newer venture, Founded, provided a digital way of creating companies, and helping entrepreneurs manage the necessary reporting for those companies. This new company, built using the feedback from their earlier experience, was able to automate and scale, which eventually led to them being acquired by RBC Ventures and merged with Ownr.[8] Honest, direct feedback or analysis isn't always easy to accept, but having a solid process in place will help reduce the risk that much bigger and often more expensive mistakes aren't made further down the road.

Receiving feedback selectively is a problem Andrew Arruda often sees. He says "Many people fall in love with a specific iteration and then use selective feedback to strengthen what they believe the prototype should be.

8. https://www.ownr.co.

Prototyping is important because it's like drawing a map to a treasure from various people who have all been around it, you're sort of collecting different puzzle pieces. If you think you have a complete map at the beginning, you're destined to fail."[9]

The issue arises when people are trying to solve a problem that they have experienced. You need to incorporate all of the feedback, even if it requires that you change your approach. Remember, you are building for many people, not just yourself.

Tips/Conclusion

There is no one way to build a prototype and guarantee the launch of a successful product or service. All we can do is make sure we take the time and follow the best process possible to give us a better chance at success.

Most of us have good ideas, yet so few of us take action on them. The lack of action is often because of the fear of failure. If you follow the design approach, invest the necessary time and energy, and take what you learn to heart, there will be an entire community of customers and advisors by your side supporting your success. Good luck!

Key Takeaways: Step 4

Prototyping is the fourth step in the design thinking process. The purpose of this step is to take your best idea from step 3 and start prototyping a minimum viable product (MVP) that you can use in step 5 to gain feedback from your target clients.

- Prototyping is as much an approach with a purpose as it is a thing. It definitely involves "creating" something, but its real value is in why you are doing it, what you find out from others (and your own reflections), and what you do as a result of that information.
- According to the Interaction Design Foundation, prototyping is "a simple experimental model of a proposed solution used to test or validate ideas, design assumptions and other aspects of its conceptualization quickly and cheaply.

9. Telephone interview with Andrew Arruda (June 14, 2021).

- The more effort you invest in prototyping on the front end, the more you are able to remove the risk from venture.
- Diversity in your team is essential. This includes diversity of thought, skills, and backgrounds.
- Always keep your focus on the problem and make sure you have deep knowledge, or are able to gain deep knowledge, around the process you are solving for.
- Match the sophistication of your prototype with the stage of solution development you're in. Examples include drawings, wireframes, and minimum viable products.
- Ask for feedback on your prototype early and often.

5

Step 5: Test and Refine: Try Your Solutions Out and Make Adjustments

Mary Juetten

As this book title includes the words, "for Lawyers Looking to Getting Things Done," this chapter is not solely design thinking theory. In fact, it's a compilation of my own and others' lessons learned with respect to testing, refining, and implementing solutions using feedback from real clients or customers. This test and refine fifth and final step means taking your solution for a test drive to identify areas of improvement, and is critical to overall success.

First, the test and refine step is predicated on the ideation and then prototype phases. Simply put, you must have a solution in some form to test with external users. Trust me, after decades in business and 12 plus years working in startups, I am not overthinking that aspect of this step. Lawyers are risk adverse, which means that the average attorney wants a perfect solution prior to any testing. More likely, a lawyer would not show a prototype to a real client for feedback. There is a fear of only having one chance to impress, and many will avoid testing with real clients and simply launch without this important test and refine step.

Second, the refining step drives an iterative process, which includes making changes based on qualitative and quantitative feedback from actual users. Some failures have come from testing that was truly just going through the motions with no intention of using the feedback to modify the offering. However, remember your refining will reach a point of diminishing returns so again you will need to balance making changes based on more testing with implementing the solution. An example of when to stop iterating with changes is in the following first solution test and refine scenario.

Third, remember that a prototype or solution is not necessarily a custom-made software product. It can take many forms: a new or automated form; new process, including manual steps; or off-the-shelf software implementation, all designed to solve the users' or clients' problems.

Design thinking is a mindset, and, like any structured change management process, you must embrace the steps and above all, remain curious, flexible, and open to possibilities.

How to Test and Refine

While the term "design thinking" is relatively new, the premise is firmly rooted in century-old management theory and decades of consulting. Luminaries like Mary Parker Follett, William Deming, and Peter Drucker, along with Masaaki Imai, laid the groundwork for the principles that are embedded in the design thinking approach.[1] In the early 1990s, as a management consultant, I used a process called Business Process Re-engineering (BPR) when I was with Price Waterhouse (predated their merger with Coopers & Lybrand to become PwC). Within BPR, Deming's Plan Do Check Act (PDCA) wheel was a key building block, and based on today's design thinking five-step approach, the PDCA influence continues. Steps one through

1. *See* Graham, Pauline. *Mary Parker Follett Prophet of Management*. Beard Books, n.d. 21 11 2022; The Deming Institute. *The PDSA Cycle (Plan-Do-Study-Act)*. n.d. 21 11 2022. https://deming.org/explore/pdsa/; Drucker, Peter. *Management: Tasks, Responsibilities, Practices*. HarperCollins, 1974. 21 11 2022. https://books.google.com/books?id=9a5SAlaY-X4C&lpg=PA84&dq=drucker%20%22planned%20abandonment%22&pg=PA84#v=onepage&q&f=false; Imai, Masaaki. *Kaizen (Ky'zen), the key to Japan's competitive success*. 1986. 21 11 2022. https://amazon.com/kaizen-key-japans-competitive-success/dp/007554332x.

four in design thinking are part of the plan phase, and then do, check, act focuses on how to test and refine in a continuous improvement setting.

Overlaying PDCA on the fifth step in design thinking, some important aspects emerge:

- Tests are on a small scale.
- Tests are controlled and monitored.
- Data is gathered as objectively as possible.

Personally, I use this PDCA approach for my continuous improvement efforts with my businesses, including my law practice, which can include new processes or product offerings and software implementation. I also focus on measurements to identify areas for improvement or problems and to validate my testing of potential solutions.

There are several different approaches to testing that depend on the status of your solution. The following apply for any type of solution or industry, including the law:

- **Alpha test.** Very early on, you may wish to ask for feedback on a prototype or solution that is only on paper or in a very rough format, usually to a select group, usually smaller than the beta test group.
- **Beta test.** An early version of automation, a software product, or a change in approach to a process is tested as either an open or closed beta test. The latter means that a group of people are invited to the test versus an open situation where you would just open the solution to all users and, in some cases, the public.
- Recently at my law firm, we explored the automation of prenuptial legal services, including intake and the draft prenuptial agreement. Before we did any design/programming in the client relationship management (CRM) software system, we did a rough process diagram and mapped out the intake information based on the prenuptial agreement. As an alpha test, we presented both the process and the intake document to family law attorneys and walked through it and made their suggested changes, all before we created the automation in our CRM. At the same law firm, we did an open beta test of the Spanish of our legal checkups by updating the website and encouraging our Spanish-speaking staff to review.

The decision between taking time to do an alpha test at an early stage is dependent on many factors. For example, when the solution is a novel or unique approach, you may wish to conduct an alpha test with a small group to determine if the full effort of creating a prototype is warranted. Likewise, the choice between open and closed beta testing is dependent on the type of change or solution.

However, the most important step is to make sure that the test group is actual users, whether that includes clients, suppliers, or the public. I have been asked several times to participate in beta testing and declined if I did not represent the true end user.

Testing and Refining Design: The First Solution

When I developed my first product for small businesses, I made some critical errors in my trial test or alpha testing as shared here.

- Asking lawyers (my advisors) to complete the testing when they were not the target end users of my software.
- Sampling too small a group to have meaningful feedback, as I ended up with several direct opposites in terms of feedback, which made it difficult to make improvements.
- Trying to test too many things at once.
- Taking feedback personally, which is hard, as a founder, to avoid.

At that time, my idea for Traklight.com was a guided questionnaire that would both gather information and educate the small business owner on potential intellectual property and necessary business steps for new or growing companies.

For my alpha test, I wrote out the questions in Excel exactly as the software would display them, like a checklist, to simulate the experience. I was looking for feedback on the questions themselves and using the responses to check my logic for the automatic report that was generated.

The simulation of the idea did show that it was useful, but I received conflicting information on which questions were understandable, and with too small a sample, I had to go back out again with revisions to a broader group. However, the idea that I could also check the logic of an auto-generated report at the same time was biting off more than I could chew.

When I moved to open beta testing, I made some new errors. Specifically, I did not spend enough time (and money) on the feedback mechanism, limiting it to a SurveyMonkey form, and I did not promote the initial website presence. However, I gained invaluable information by talking to various users and by later extending the free period to some local incubators and other small businesses.

During the refine step, we had significant internal debate about how much to change before the questionnaire was ready to release again. For example, we changed all the wording that users identified as unclear or ambiguous. Also, user feedback identified that there were too many introductory questions on one screen that required scrolling and needed to be grouped in logical shorter sections. We refined the first section into four main sections and then broke down the last planning section into four subsections. There was a positive response to the new structure, and it actually remains today. However, a couple of users suggested moving the questions between sections, but we decided that there was no value to making those changes.

Setting a road map for your project is critical, so that the right balance is struck between improvements and the diminishing returns of changes where the cost of the change exceeds the additional value. That said, we continue to gather feedback and make changes to this day.

Other approaches for testing and refining solutions include formal and informal focus groups, trial free periods, free portions of a service or product. In the foreword, Jess Birken talked about her informal individual testing process as she implemented an online scheduling solution. While approaches can range from the formal large-scale to an individual's random testing, all need to have an execution plan and metrics as discussed later.

However, it's worth stating, "better done than perfect" when it comes to testing and refining.

Testing and Refining Design: Who's the Customer

A brief note before we dive into some more case studies. As I learned, it's important to understand your ultimate customer or client when designing a test or deciding to make an improvement. I am referring to who will be using the new solution—is it for your administrative staff, for lawyers, for the public, for business owners, and or others? In some cases, the answer may include more than one category of user.

Although I am a proponent of client-centered or customer-centered legal services delivery, you must design for your user. Sounds simple but, unfortunately, we often instead design for ourselves, which can lead to solutions tested and refined with the wrong audience.

A few years ago, when I was on the board of a legal quasi-trade association, we were implementing a chat bot with frequently asked questions (FAQs) for the website. The organization's mission talked about promoting access to justice for all, particularly the underserved. Our implementation was hampered by the fact that the chat bot was not for the public, but rather for potential lawyer members. At the board level, we did not take the time to design the test of the solution and have lawyers run through both the FAQs and the process, instead relying on administrative folks. We could have saved time by involving a few lawyers in the testing, particularly those that are not as familiar with technology.

Currently, I am a co-founder of Singular Law Group, a new Alternative Business Structure (ABS) law firm in Arizona. We use several lead generation tools that are client-facing, including the Traklight legal checks provided for individuals and businesses, but more on that later. In the process of automating the intake process, including the engagement letter, we recognized that the users will be lawyers and administrative personnel. As we design and test the process flow, we have planned weekly check-ins as the process is rolled out to the attorneys in a step-by-step manner. We set up the tests after understanding each attorney's level of technology sophistication. Just like with legal service delivery, it's important to meet the user at their comfort level during the testing stage to ensure that the solutions are workable.

Testing And Refining Design: A Process Improvement Cautionary Tale

Prior to launching Singular Law Group, I was involved in an overseas consulting project where we worked on process improvement, using the six sigma approach. One of my consulting projects involved an overhaul of an administrative system for hiring that crossed multiple departments.

Following the six sigma methodology, we gained stakeholder and project sponsor approval prior to scheduling multiple workshops over months where we prepared and analyzed plus flushed out bottlenecks. However, after identifying the top priorities in each stream and developing solutions, we were blocked from testing the improvements.

We went back through the stakeholder engagement process and the notes from the meetings, and, at all times, the full team had agreed upon the changes outlined in the project charter. When we went deeper and actually interviewed the people blocking the testing, it turned out that they were told to participate and did not truly believe in the change effort. Although this was an extreme case, it highlights the importance of ensuring that everyone involved in your project, regardless of scale or size, must be committed to change.

Testing and Refining Design: Avoiding Shelf-ware

For those lawyers who are creating software or automating documents as a solution, it's critical to not only test and refine with respect to operability but also to ensure that the surrounding process is examined, tested, and tweaked to ensure adoption. This brings up the need for identification of and buy-in by all stakeholders, from the beginning. For small projects, particularly those done by individuals, this buy-in and the planning can be more informal. However, for major undertakings, a project road map (also called a charter) is important for several reasons.

Foremost, a project charter forces a plan and review of the process, proposed solutions, and outcomes with all the interested stakeholders. When developing and reviewing with your team and interested parties, it's important to assess whether everyone is committed to the project. Managing change is a critical piece of any project and even if you move through all five steps, your solution may not gain traction if there is resistance (see the sidebar for a cautionary tale).

The charter provides a reference document for all those involved and should also include a testing plan plus metrics to measure implementation success. In addition, when guiding the team, a project manager can use the charter to remind stakeholders of the objectives and their commitment to change.

Several years ago, we sold and implemented Traklight's software to a thirty-partner law firm as a business checkup and intellectual property (IP) identification and tracking software for small businesses. The firm ran an inhouse startup incubator and the Traklight business risk assessment yielded employment, security, and privacy law matters, in addition to business and IP law leads.

In short, Traklight's software is designed to be used by the business or inventor, who creates a road map and receives a dashboard evaluation of their business risk plus links and a report for next steps. The experience is to educate the client and provide a live version of their checkup to be updated regularly. On the lawyer side, the software provides automated lead generation in the form of a "snapshot" report that is instantly emailed to the attorney (or anyone at the firm) with all the potential client's questions and answers. Basically, the leads are generated while the potential clients are educated on their needs; the lawyers do not have to use their time or do a free consultation to learn about the potential clients' issues.

However, even though we met numerous times with the firm, and the partners all expressed support for the software implementation, there was very little actual use. In fact, after some time, we canceled the contract with the firm because it felt wrong to take their money. Part of this "shelf-ware" issue was that the partners could not agree on making changes to their process to include Traklight's software. Also, of the several testers for the implementation, two partners spent months debating the disclaimer and wanted changes to the standard questions. We definitely fell into a test and refine endless loop and that caused the initial enthusiasm among the lawyers to wan considerably before the launch. However, the lack of buy-in to include a link to complete the quick ten-minute questionnaire as part of the engagement process and the resistance to placing a free business legal checkup on their website doomed the project.

Fast forward to Singular Law Group, where Traklight is part of the lead generation process and is on the website as a free checkup for individuals and businesses. As we started testing the version of Traklight created for Singular Law Group, we realized that we needed to have the software available in Spanish for our potential clients. During testing we did notice that our quick verbatim version in Spanish is too long for some of the questions in the checkup. In an example of better done than perfect (and an open beta test as outlined earlier), the translated version of Traklight is now on the live site but it's on my to-do list to have it reworded in Spanish to be shorter and therefore display better on a phone or iPad.

Final Note on Test and Refine: Measurement

As part of the overall running of a law firm, an in-house legal department, or any business, metrics are important. Specific to the test and refine phase, a check on the viability or feasibility of a solution is usually measured both quantitively and qualitatively. Whether that is to measure the impact of a solution or customer satisfaction with a change, key performance metrics (KPIs) should be set for the project early on. These metrics should be a good blend of numbers and qualitative feedback. Traditional numeric metrics may include looking at the impact of a new solution on collections, profitability, process time, non-billable time, and so on.

As an example of a blend of numbers and feedback in a less traditional approach within the law, a simple net promoter score (NPS) can be used to measure the impact of a new solution. If you have been doing NPS all along, you can simply gather new scores during the test period and compare results to those from before the new solution.

If you are not doing NPS, you can implement using SurveyMonkey by asking: How likely are you to recommend <fill in service or firm> to your friends, family, or colleagues on a scale of one to ten, with ten being extremely likely and one being not at all likely. And then add the question "Why or why not?" with an area to provide a written answer.

The NPS calculation divides the scores into the following categories:

Promoter—9 or 10

Neutral—7 or 8

Detractor—1 to 6

To calculate the NPS score, subtract the percentage of detractors from the percentage of promoters, ignoring the neutrals. The range of NPS scores is from –100 to 100, the latter occurring if everyone is a promoter (9 or 10). The significance of the NPS score can be in the absolute number or in a trend over time as you test and refine.

Two areas of contention for using NPS; first fatigue from surveys is very real. However, within the law, the NPS approach is relatively new. Second, there is also some debate over whether an NPS survey should be anonymous, but in my opinion you would wish to follow up on any qualitative comments, even during the testing stage.

Often the best feedback comes from the answers to the "why or why not" question, whether this is done during testing or regular operations. During testing, the information provided by target users can inform refinements.

Testing and Refining Design: Lessons Learned

The preceding experiences have provided valuable input into our approach to the creation of Singular Law Group, particularly as we automate forms, engagement letters, and processes.

And remember "better done than perfect." You can always be improving using a continuous feedback loop and the agile method plus of course design thinking, whether it's software, a document, or a process.

Key Takeaways: Step 5

This is the fifth and final step in the design thinking process. The purpose of this step is to take the prototype you created in step 4 and use it to gain feedback from your target clients. Use the feedback you receive to refine the solution. Continue this process and refine.

- Make sure that you are designing and testing solutions that meet the users at their comfort level and in the place where they would normally interact.
- For major projects or changes, find an internal sponsor to help with any roadblocks for testing and refining (and the whole project actually!).
- Develop an agreed upon road map or project charter that leaves some flexibility to react to feedback.
- Come up with the evaluation framework and related metrics for your solution early and do not be afraid to change as you refine.

PART II

Putting It All Together

Marching through the steps of the design thinking process, how would you apply this model to your firm tomorrow? Next week? Don't let the perfect be the enemy of the good! Follow along here to see how to apply the steps to a single aspect of your firm—customer service—that can have a resounding effect.

6

Creating Exceptional Customer Service

Jim Calloway

Years ago, I gave a presentation in several jurisdictions called the Client-Centered Law Practice. It focused on the irony that law firms, at least in theory, completely revolved around serving the clients and appropriately addressing the clients' legal needs, while clients sometimes had an impression that greatly differed from that. To those clients, it seemed like the law firm was busily engaged in doing really important work for very important people while their matter was not a priority.

In fairness to lawyers, that was frequently the perception rather than reality. But in the legal world your client's perception often *is* your reality. Certainly, it is your reality where concerns like client retention, clients referring others to the firm, and complaints about law firms to others is involved.

Designing a law practice that provides exceptional client service should be the goal of every lawyer in private practice. But it does require recognition that accomplishing a great result for the client's legal problem, a goal most lawyers are equipped to provide, differs from providing good client service.

Suppose the lawyer negotiates a settlement of a claim for $10,000 more than their highest estimate of its value. The lawyer is thrilled at the outstanding accomplishment. The client, however, may have their assessment clouded by the number of times they waited several days for the lawyer to return a telephone call or still remember the in-person appointment with the lawyer that started 15 minutes late and was then cut short because the lawyer had a court appearance.

What about receiving a far better than predicted settlement? Once a client is critical of a lawyer's credibility or performance, it is easy to assume the lawyer was just "low balling" that initial estimate, or assume that because the lawyer didn't get that dramatic "gotcha" moment of the opposing party in court, that the lawyer had not acted effectively or competently.

Weak customer service practices impact every aspect of a lawyer's representation of a client, including weakening the client's confidence and trust in the lawyer.

In terms of perception versus reality, lawyers need to appreciate or at least keep an open mind to the possibility that how clients prefer to receive legal services today is not in line with what lawyers believe that they prefer.

An Empathetic Approach

We are all consumers of goods and services and we can all empathize with poor consumer service, whether it is waiting in an office for a long time after your scheduled appointment or providers not doing things as they said they would when they said they would.

But there's a certain amount of empathy that is more challenging for many in our profession to realize. Having others now in control of very important and personal aspects of our lives can't help but be personal. Being forced to discuss your marital problems and your recent history with a stranger is hard. This is true even though the stranger may be committed to helping you cope with your problems. After all, that lawyer could have just as easily been hired by your adversary. In a time when many people often are frustrated by a lack of control over their lives, this is an important point. Your empathetic approach and understanding must be flexible. Dealing with a person who has been an abused spouse or who has a history of deprivation and poverty may merit someone highlighting the control that they still have in their current circumstances, while representing a corporate executive or powerful lawyer who is very frustrated by their current lack of power may require a somewhat different approach.

Understanding what your clients want in terms of their legal service delivery is a prerequisite to delivering services in that manner.

Defining the Problem(s)

The second step of design thinking is to define the problem. For legal services delivery, there are several intertwined problems.

- The situation needing resolution that has generated this client engagement
- The lawyer delivering a solution to the problem that is both affordable for the client and produces profitable revenue for the law firm
- The subjective belief of the client as to the appropriateness of the legal remedies proposed

But the design challenge for the law firm we will discuss here is delivering legal services effectively and affordably in a way that assures the client their matter is being handled diligently and professionally while they are always informed about the matter's status and the next steps ahead.

Ideate

It is important to engage everyone who works in the law firm to brainstorm creative solutions that might improve law office operations. The lawyer's view of what is most frustrating to clients during the representation process may be different from the law firm receptionist's view and there's a good chance that the receptionist's view may be more accurate in some aspects.

Data is important in any business improvement enterprise. The best source of data related to your law firm's client experience is from former clients of the law firm. Post-representation surveys, exit interviews, and other techniques can solicit input from your past clients to improve future clients' representation. One does want to encourage clients to pass along any criticism or frustration that they experienced. One good way to solicit these responses is to ask questions like "What is the best thing that our law firm did during your representation?" and "What is an area where we can improve?"

It is also important to appreciate that different types of clients have different expectations. The primary distinction between types of clients involves the differences between business/corporate clients and individual clients, sometimes called the "people law" sector.

Business clients often have a general counsel or assistant general counsel that is assigned to monitor the representation. Reports and communications in that scenario are lawyer to lawyer and differ greatly from representing an individual who is not familiar with the legal system. If the lawyer is often tardy on deadlines or unavailable to the assistant general counsel for inquiries, there's a good chance that the client may seek other counsel in the future. Keeping the general counsel updated and involved is a good formula to obtain repeat engagements from the client.

Individual clients hiring a lawyer to deal with a personal problem often are experiencing angst, uncertainty, fear, and other negative emotions. The empathetic approach for these clients should be focused on assuring the client their lawyer "has their back" and that they should let their lawyer do the worrying for them now. Reducing uncertainly for these clients means that every time one task or step is accomplished, the client is quickly informed of what is next.

A key to representing someone unfamiliar with the legal process is to provide them with understandable and clear explanations of exactly what the situation is and the possibilities for the future. But it's also important that the representation be affordable, and billing clients for one size fits all general explanations of the legal process are inferior to videos, handouts, information available in client portals, and other tools that can help bring the client up to speed without receiving a bill from the lawyer. In fact, it may become more common to have clients watch a brief video before meeting with the lawyer to help them refine their questions.

Prototype and Testing

Once a new method or model has been developed, then the benefit is proved by actual client experiences. The law firm staff can test to see how they are impacted. Hopefully, you will develop processes that are automated and provide great client services without an additional amount of staff time being committed.

But the final and only appropriate judge of how your improvement efforts have succeeded is the experience of the clients themselves. And to obtain that information you must solicit the clients' feedback.

Now let's discuss some of the major areas that are often ripe for improvement.

Client Communications

No matter how much energy is devoted to examining and ideation of law firm improvements, it is most likely that many of the improvements will be related to attempting to improve the law firm's client communication. Many of the challenges in the attorney-client relationship are caused by poor communication practices. Even if they are not caused by poor communication, the primary way to address the challenges is often through improved communication practices.

Digital technology has shaped consumers' viewpoints of what timely service delivery is. Before email, the delivery of the Postal Service mail each day defined some of the law firm's tasks and responses for that day. But now information flows into the office throughout the day and evening. There should be some 24/7 method of dealing with client communications even when there is no one available at the firm. Email operates constantly as well. Online client portals are one primary tool for accomplishing this. Clients often feel better about logging in and posting queries to the portal as opposed to just sending an email.

At a minimum, all clients should always know the status of their matter and what should be happening next. The client intake process should cover the ways the client has to communicate with the law firm and also create expectations as to how quickly responses to communications will be made. But to excel at being client centered, opportunities for client input at appropriate stages in the proceeding are critically important. Client input is required when important decisions affecting the matter are being made. Retaining these important communications is important to protect the law firm as well.

Clients should be entitled to receive communication in a method that is appropriate and useful to them. But the law firm must securely communicate in a manner that protects client confidentiality. This tension should be addressed at an early stage in the proceeding. Often the client will have to make some adjustments to the law firms preferred communication methods.

Likewise, the firm must be open to adjusting its model when it does not adequately serve client needs. For example, if a law firm represents a number of long-haul drivers who communicate primarily by text message and rarely check their email, then the firm may have to explore incorporating text messages into its client communication process and explore the enterprise texting tools that will facilitate proper retention of those records.

Automation

Automation wouldn't have ranked high on any list of law firms needs just a few years ago. But today a law firm should incorporate current automation tools to facilitate client services without incurring either unnecessary billable hours or law firm staff time. Your client portal should be configured so when new documents are uploaded, a notice of the new document availability is automatically sent out to the client. Templates should be created for important client communications that happen regularly in the same way that templates should be created for legal documents that are frequently used. Modifications may be required. But having the task 90 percent done when you began is a benefit for everyone.

Lawyers often struggle with having enough time to do everything that they have to accomplish. When that happens, the lawyers appropriately focus on court-mandated deadlines and other matters that could hurt a client's cause. Client communication must sometimes be deferred when that happens. The more routine administrative tasks you can automate within your firm, the less likely this will occur.

Managing Clients' Expectations

Many clients have no appreciation of how much time certain legal processes involving courts and government agencies take to accomplish. This is particularly true if their main exposure to the law is watching television dramas where the crime, investigation, arrest, and trial all occur within the same episode.

Law firms, on the other hand, appreciate the time for processes in their jurisdiction and it should be an important part of the law firm client intake process to help establish the client's expectations as to how rapidly their legal matter may take to be resolved. If the prospective client is unwilling to accept the reality of the limitations of the system and has impossible demands at intake, it is better to let the prospective client seek other counsel now than to have the unhappy client fire the law firm midway through the representation.

Normally, it won't come to that. But it's far better to explain in advance the number of telephone calls that the law firm receives and that the firm's policy of returning phone messages within 48 hours after they are received is done so the lawyers can do what they promise they will. Certainly, there may be times that the client will get a return call within the hour, but you want to prepare the client in advance for when that will not be possible, and also provide them with alternative methods of communication in the event of an emergency, like the name and phone number of the legal assistant who is assigned to the case.

It can also be important to explain in advance how many digital methods of communication are not secure and the ramifications of information being exposed so the client appreciates why the law firm insists on utilizing secure communications tools.

Transparency

The need for greater transparency is often associated with governmental entities.

It is certainly not necessary to sketch out every aspect of how representation should proceed during the initial interview process. But once the client has retained the firm, the goal should be a clear road map so everyone understands the steps involved. Certainly, many legal matters will not follow a standard process when unusual developments occur. But when a client is upset about delays, it can be very helpful to go to the original road map provided to the client and indicate where these types of delays were suggested as a possibility.

It is also appropriate to note in a friendly nonjudgmental way when the client's actions or inactions have contributed to a delay. Transparency should go both directions.

Respect the Client's Time as Much as You Want Them to Respect Your Time

Whether it is the waiting room for a doctor or a lawyer, no one likes being seated in the waiting room 20 or 30 minutes after their scheduled appointment. There was a time when clients were more tolerant of this, but today the law firm must exert great effort to make sure that clients are seen at their scheduled appointment time or within ten minutes afterwards. This should be an articulated goal contained in the plan for making the law firm's process delivery more client centered.

People tend to have a more limited attention span for reading lengthy material today. If it is necessary to provide the client with a lengthy document or memo explaining a legal position or theory, perhaps the firm should consider the corporate communication method of beginning these documents with a short executive summary.

What Is Your Exceptional Client Service Model?

Every law firm is different. A law firm that serves mainly consumers differs from a firm that serves mainly businesses and corporate clients. A firm in a certain geographical region will no doubt reflect the values and culture of that region. Some things that might work for other law firms may not work for yours.

Therefore, every law firm must seek its own path forward. But consumer attitudes are changing and exceptional client service is one area where the cliche of "failing to plan is planning to fail" may be an appropriate warning.

But beware of one law firm mantra that will impair success in redesigning your law firm: "But we've never done it that way before." This is the time in private practice where it is very appropriate to experiment and try new approaches even if this is not in the tradition of how many law firms have operated in the past.

Jack Newton, CEO and co-founder of practice management software provider Clio, in his 2020 book *The Client-Centered Law Firm* identified five major values of a client-centered law firm approach:

1. Developing deep client empathy
2. Practicing attentiveness
3. Providing ease of communications between lawyer and client
4. Demanding effortless experiences
5. Creating clients for life

What are the major values you want your client-centered law firm to prioritize? First steps are important. Improving customer service should be an ongoing project for the law firm. But don't let the magnitude of change prevent your law firm from getting started. Your clients deserve your best, and less anxious clients make things better both for the clients and those working in your firm.

PART III

Real World Examples

Now that you are familiar with the five steps of design thinking and have seen examples of how it can be used in a customer service context, let's see how it can be applied to create or improve a service, product, or process. This section will introduce you to the following five real-world case examples:

1. The Law Shop, by AJ Skogerson and Andrea McGinn
2. Reimagine the Client Journey in Litigation, by Ginevra Saylor
3. Immigration Law, by Greg Siskind
4. Online Courses, by Lisa Feldstein
5. Wills and Estate Planning Software, by Jordan M. Atin

The examples are varied and meant to illustrate a wide range of design thinking use cases. Some of the authors were familiar with the concept of design thinking and intentionally applied it in the examples you will read. Others were not and instead intuitively moved through the steps. After reading these examples, you may discover that you are already in the latter camp!

The first case example illustrates how AJ Skogerson and Andrea McGinn used design thinking to create The Law Shop, their client-centric law firm offering primary unbundled services—a win-win for clients and lawyers. The second case example illustrates how Ginevra Saylor's firm, Gowling WLG (Canada) LLP, used design thinking to reimage the client journey in litigation with the goal of streamlining the process, delivering greater value, and enhancing overall client satisfaction. The third case example illustrates how Greg Siskind used design thinking to create technology solutions that resolved various client and law firm pain points. The fourth case example illustrates how Lisa Feldstein used design thinking to develop online courses to make access to legal information more accessible and maintain an active client pipeline.

And finally, the fifth case example illustrates how Jordan M. Atin used design thinking to build a legal software solution to enhance client experience and reduce risks when drafting wills.

We hope these examples will get your creative juices flowing and inspire you to consider how you can use design thinking to create or improve a service, product, or process in your practice.

7

Applying the Steps: The Law Shop

AJ Skogerson and Andrea McGinn

The concept of "access to justice" has been a hot topic among professional legal organizations and at continuing education programs around the globe for some time. Attorneys who now offer "unbundled legal services" to their clients on a regular basis are resolving many of the concerns related to access to justice for all. Those same attorneys are finding that adapting their practices to provide legal services on a limited scope basis at times provides wonderful personal and professional benefits for attorneys and law firms as well.

In 2017, we co-founded The Law Shop by Skogerson McGinn LLC (TLS). In just a few short years, TLS has become a globally recognized leader in developing a law firm of the future. TLS is an exclusively unbundled, private practice law firm proving daily that it's possible to provide high-quality legal services to almost any individual who comes in the door without sacrificing the health and well-being of the firm's attorneys or the profitability of the business.

Empathize

Prior to founding TLS, we were office mates and solo attorneys of differing generations, though we had a similar desire to always work with parties and colleagues we encountered positively and respectfully. Our relatively traditional law practices were typical and successful by most attorney standards. Yet individuals within our community needing help with common legal matters were still plagued with the baggage presently associated with finding quality legal representation, such as:

- Ever-increasing cost of traditional legal representation
- Inability or (understandable) unwillingness to pay significant retainer fees
- Legal aid and other low-income options being too full or having too many conflicts to assist in a timely manner, if at all
- Spotty online DIY resources combined with lack of understanding as to laws applicable in the relevant jurisdiction versus elsewhere
- Decreasing number of legal professionals in rural areas
- Lack of access to basic legal information and/or guidance without payment of a sizeable retainer fee up front
- Finding counsel with the bandwidth to take on cases involving complex legal issues
- No options for legal assistance other than full scope attorney representation

In addition to the challenges faced by community members needing legal help, we, the local legal professionals, had our own list of stressors associated with traditional private practice: unrelenting personal stress; guilt over not being able to provide affordable legal assistance to more individuals; feast or famine mindset, especially in a small firm where income is generated by just one or a few individuals; high firm overhead; lack of work-life balance; pressure to be constantly available to clients and colleagues; potential ethical violations; keeping up with technology; attorney burnout; and much more.

The more we thought and talked about these challenges with each other and with our colleagues, the more we came to believe that there had to be a way to change the existing system. We needed to take a step back and assess how we could more meaningfully help people of all socioeconomic backgrounds and do so without sacrificing so much of ourselves in the process. At the time, it seemed almost shameful in the practice of law, particularly in the area of family law, for attorneys to have dual goals—to help people *and* make a good living while doing it. The general sense within the legal community was often a presumption of misery among seasoned practitioners. Fortunately, we have now found that such presumption can actually be kicked to the curb entirely through the effective use of unbundled legal services.

Define (the Problem)

Consider the following common case examples:

> **Example 1:** Potential Client (PC) comes to your office for an initial consultation. PC's case involves numerous complex and/or high-conflict issues. PC's small budget for legal services has caused multiple other attorneys to turn down PC's case already. PC was referred to you by Legal Aid because although PC's budget is small, PC does not qualify for pro bono legal services. PC seems like a great person and you would like to help, but you can already see the amount of time and work that would be required of you in handling every aspect of PC's case. You know PC's initial retainer fee would be gone in the first month of your representation and that is presuming more issues do not arise from PC's already tenuous situation.
>
> **Example 2:** PC comes to your office for an initial consultation in a divorce. PC is a very high-income earner, as is PC's spouse. Both hold ownership interests in the businesses where they work. You advised PC that the parties' business interests should be valued by a financial professional, but PC tells you neither he nor PC's spouse want to have valuations completed. The two get along well and have already worked through most, if not all, of their case issues together on their own. They just want help ensuring the proper documents are prepared and shuttled through the court system in the right order at the right times. You know PC can easily afford to retain you for full-service representation, but PC and PC's spouse

have agreed upon a budget for completing their divorce that is considerably less than your usual minimum retainer fee for full representation.

Scenarios such as these yield the same understandable concern on the part of both litigants and lawyers: MONEY. Under each of these examples and at least a hundred others, the lawyer could and likely does desire to do the work. However, the potential client either cannot or will not compensate the attorney adequately for the work the attorney would be obligated to complete under a traditional full representation model, that is, providing *unlimited* legal representation. In contrast, if we utilized *limited* scope representation in each of these scenarios, we could provide extremely valuable services for these clients by focusing only on moving them *forward* and by agreeing to where our services can be the most effective at a cost that works for both the client and the attorney.

The rough statistics regarding self-represented litigants these days are staggering. Though extensive studies have to date been few and far between, we learned through industry leaders such as Forrest Mosten and others, as well as our own research, that the majority of litigants in family law matters are now without legal representation. And many of those litigants *can* afford some level of legal representation, yet they are intentionally going it alone in the court system. Judges and clerks of court in our own state have shared that our court system is drowning in self-represented litigants and has been doing so for at least ten years now.

What is driving this tidal wave of self-representation? From what we've been able to gather, here are some of the most common reasons:

- Attorney cost, even for the wealthy
- Limited capacity of legal aid organizations
- Negative public perception of lawyers generally
- Major growth of online legal services
- Increased consumer preference for digital and DIY alternatives

A general lack of options somewhere between high-cost full representation and largely unavailable pro bono representation under the added weight of the foregoing factors is preventing otherwise potential clients of all socioeconomic backgrounds from even bothering to consult with a local attorney before venturing into the court system solo. How do we, as attorneys, educate the public about the incredible value of our own services if we can't even get clients in the door? And how do we get clients in the door without losing substantial revenues while meeting with folks who either can't or won't retain us for full representation?

Ideate

We became interested in exploring the use of unbundled legal services within our firm because we wanted to help people, but we were also just plain tired. Our colleagues expressed feeling the same. Together we had attended a few brief continuing education sessions at out-of-state seminars on unbundled services. This form of practice seemed to offer the option for continuing to provide high quality legal services while also having some actual choice in the kind of work we enjoyed and wanted to do versus tasks we either didn't enjoy, didn't have time for, or didn't feel especially proficient at. Except for the few folks on the national scene, most of our colleagues thought of unbundled legal services as the fastest way to lose our own shorts. Thus, if we were going to make a real go of it with an unbundled practice, we needed to spend time establishing systems and processes for covering all the bases—ethical rules, marketing, client onboarding, and, most especially, identifying and pricing the services we would offer.

We had both handled a fair number of real estate matters, a practice area in which it is common for specific attorney tasks to be priced on a flat fee basis associated with attorney time and/or transaction value. We were also both trained and experienced in the collaborative process for family law matters, giving us some foundation for talking with clients about limiting the scope of our representation in at least one major way—representation without litigation. As we became more comfortable dialoguing with our clients about excluding litigation in a collaborative divorce setting, we were pleasantly surprised to learn that most of our clients actually loved the idea of having an attorney who had fully explained the legal process and then provided an option for that process that excluded litigation. A discussion we thought would cause angst for potential clients turned out to have the opposite effect—it actually made our clients feel more confident about the quality of the representation they expected to receive.

Both the real estate services and collaborative representation just noted involve "unbundled legal services" a.k.a. "limited scope representation" (LSR). With LSR, we are simply breaking a legal matter up into parts and pieces, pricing those parts and pieces by average time and/or value, and then discussing those parts and pieces with our clients so as to reach agreement regarding what we will handle and for how much. In essence, every client is given license to "choose your own adventure." Likewise, the attorney has license to refine his or her service offerings to include ONLY the kinds of work the attorney truly enjoys, prefers doing, or currently has the time and bandwidth to handle.

Prototype

If we were going to make a fully unbundled legal services firm truly work in a private practice law firm, we had some significant obstacles to overcome. Since the inception of limited scope representation, such services have largely been touted by professional and charitable organizations as something that attorneys can do to help the underprivileged. Yet, despite public perception to the contrary, most lawyers already *do* a massive amount of work to help folks of lesser means and there are limits—physically, emotionally, and financially—to how much free legal work attorneys can do while also maintaining their own health and well-being, supporting their own families, and maintaining businesses that employ others. This is why we decided that instead of looking at unbundled legal services as a way to help only struggling clients, such services might actually be a way to help *everyone*—struggling clients *and* struggling lawyers. The plan we developed included:

- **Mission.** Help our clients, our colleagues, and ourselves to live our very best lives.
- **Legal authority.** Rules of ethics and civil procedure, especially the latter. In reading these authorities, we focused on what they said we *could* do rather than what we couldn't.
- **Starting point.** Breaking up a case from start to finish, focusing on the individual tasks and phases associated with a typical family law matter. At TLS, this initially involved creating an a la carte menu of services and service packages with prices based primarily on our

usual hourly rate and the average time needed to complete common tasks. (Sidebar: You get to craft your unbundled services in whatever way works best for you!)

- **Brand.** "The Law Shop"—a retail bookstore theme that is easy for lawyers to market and for the public to remember.
  - Tagline: "Let us help you turn the page."
  - Marketing: Primarily organic, including positive, original social media content; strategically placed informational brochures; plenty of firm swag for employees, family, and friends; active involvement in professional organizations; public speaking engagements; attorney and staff workshops; charitable contributions and sponsorships; and so on.
- **Buyer persona.** A new target market—the majority of family law litigants now choosing or being forced to go it alone. Focusing on this particular market provided the added bonus of effectively removing TLS from having to compete with the majority of other law firms still going after the minority of family law litigants with the ability and willingness to spend large sums on legal fees.
- **Client pitch.** At TLS, clients have *options.* We start most potential clients with a Shop Evaluation, which is a 40-minute paid consultation with three distinct phases:
  - *Client's story*—potential client's opportunity to tell a TLS attorney about this particular chapter of his or her life story, that is, the client's legal matter.
  - *General legal process*—attorney provides the client with a 30,000 foot view of the beginning, middle, and end of the legal process.
  - *TLS service options*[1]—discussion of the options available to the client for legal services at various levels based on agreed upon goals and budget.
- **Lawyer pitch.** Unbundled legal services reduce attorney stress and increase a firm's bottom line.

1. Consistently providing all clients with all options allows for both maximum informed consent and additional marketing through clients serving as mini firm ambassadors with their own families and friends.

Test

Let's circle back to Examples 1 and 2. How might we now approach each of these scenarios using a limited scope approach? At first glance, these cases look messy, possibly quite expensive, and/or fraught with potential ethical concerns. Yet if we step back, take a deep breath, and look at the variety of ways in which we could simply move the clients *forward*. . .

Example 1: The core issue for both the client and the attorney in this matter is money. The client lacks it, and the attorney needs it to do the job. On an unbundled basis, an attorney could:

- Reach out to the other party's attorney to negotiate an agreement as to payment of both parties' attorney fees from joint funds
- File a request with the court for a hearing to determine an award of attorney fees that would allow your client to proceed with further representation
- Assist the client with the preparation and filing of a response to the pending legal action and/or an appropriate pre-answer motion
- Draft agreed upon documents for the client and then provide the client with template instructions for filing his or her own court documents
- Provide coaching services only

Example 2: In this scenario, money for legal fees is not a key concern for the parties. They feel they have done their own due diligence and they are now looking for an attorney who will honor the deal and the budget they reached on their own. On an unbundled basis, an attorney could:

- Have the parties execute a conflict waiver solely for the purpose of allowing the attorney to provide a paid spousal education session regarding unbundled legal service options for moving forward
- Draft all the necessary documents for the client's legal matter including a provision in the parties' settlement agreement that acknowledges and waives the right to further discovery

and/or due diligence; refer the unrepresented party to an unbundled attorney in another firm to review and discuss the documents with such party prior to signing; and then timely file the documents with the court
- Direct the parties to pro se litigant tools available within the jurisdiction and provide coaching services for proper use of such tools

Over time, we have learned that each one of these suggested approaches can be a valid solution to helping the client simply move *forward*. It is up to the attorneys to provide the options, and then our clients get to choose from those options or go elsewhere, something it turns out they rarely ever do. All of these approaches can be offered on an hourly or flat fee basis with payment required in advance of the service(s) being provided. Though we typically suggest specific options that might be a good fit, clients can and often do surprise us by choosing a form of representation other than what we recommended or expected, which lines up well with the concept of informed consent. Unbundled clients have much more realistic expectations in relation to the service(s) they will be receiving from the attorney. They are more cautious about their use of our time and their money. They are often happy to retain us for additional services should the need arise, signing a new updated services agreement and paying a new flat or retainer fee up front in advance of such additional services.

By the time we officially launched TLS, we were confident that the new, limited scope service options being offered at TLS would quickly gain favor with clients, and they did. Convincing other lawyers that unbundled is the ticket to lower stress and higher income, on the other hand, was a much more daunting task. Iowa had no existing playbook for how to actually create an entire law firm around limited-scope representation and almost no precedence for use of the relevant rules of ethics and civil procedure. Local judges were extremely supportive of the concept but were unable to offer any experienced advice or wisdom.

We could appreciate the hesitation within our own profession. Aside from the existing popular myth that limited scope work is solely for helping poor people, lawyers are highly trained specialists who are bred from law school on to feel and be responsible for every aspect of a client's case. We work tremendously hard to take care of our clients, sometimes at the cost of our own personal relationships, pocketbooks, and even mental health. We are also deathly afraid of unintentionally committing an ethical violation with the potential to destroy a career we worked so hard to build. Our laser focus on liability, putting the client first, and keeping our firms afloat explains why so many attorneys look at unbundled legal services and see only certain financial loss and looming ethical violations.

Like most of our colleagues, we had experienced all the same concerns, yet the idea of not having to handle every aspect of every client's case was just too tantalizing to pass up, so we planned carefully and then took the leap. Once we had proven it truly is possible to build an exclusively unbundled legal services firm, we no longer needed to work to convince our colleagues of the viability of this concept. They could see that our clients were still getting excellent service, our attorneys were more relaxed, well compensated, and have greater work-life balance. We now offer consistently sold out workshops on unbundled legal services and we have a significant and growing number of unbundled practitioners in our own geographic area that we are thrilled to see and with whom we love networking!

Lawyers at TLS have now become experts at "exercising their 'no' muscles," which means gently declining to engage further when a client tries to pull the lawyer in for work outside the scope of the client's current services agreement. This is not to say additional services cannot or will not be provided. To the contrary, most clients actually appreciate and respect a gentle reminder of the previously agreed upon boundaries within the client's case. Clients are very often willing to execute a new legal services agreement with corresponding fees to obtain additional assistance if desired.

Over time, we continuously assess and adapt our firm's systems, processes, forms, and use of technology as new and better ideas are developed to adapt to our consistently increasing volume of clients and attorneys. Some examples include:

- Establishing strong gatekeeping practices for staff and attorneys.
- Creating and utilizing time-saving forms and templates for efficient case management.
- Meeting with colleagues, business consultants, and other professionals on a continuing basis to gain knowledge from others we admire and want to learn from.

- Switching from a somewhat overwhelming a la carte menu to a simple "table of contents" visual aid showing four general service categories that can then be customized on a case-by-case basis.
- Weaving The Law Shop brand into nearly every aspect of our firm, including our legal services agreements that incorporate terms such as "character," "setting," "plot," and even "royalties." Though these ideas might seem silly to some, they have helped us to clearly establish our own memorable and modern brand within our community.
- Developing a streamlined client onboarding process accessible through our website, saving tremendous staff time, which helps us avoid having to hire additional employees unnecessarily.
- Utilizing online scheduling services.
- Embracing the value that financial, mental health, and other professionals can bring to client matters in ways lawyers cannot.
- Encouraging clients to explore mediation, collaborative practice, and other consensual dispute resolution options prior to filing an action with the court.
- Increasing prices based more on the value of the work than on the time per task. Clients are often happy to pay a premium for a legal service when they know exactly how much they will pay and exactly what service(s) they will be getting.
- Ensuring use of neutrally stated pleadings and other documents whenever possible so as to minimize the possibility of increasing animosity between the parties and decreasing the likelihood of timely settlement.
- Giving a client homework on his or her own case, being proactive with client appointments, and having established access points for the client at predetermined stages of his or her case.
- Requiring a new or updated signed legal services agreement describing the work to be performed and agreed upon payment arrangement prior to the commencement of any work on the client's case.
- Filing limited appearances in all cases that specifically identify the work to be performed by the attorney and other relevant information.
- Conversing regularly with our clients and own team members to get their feedback and input on any way in which we can improve the services we provide.

Still Writing Our Own Story

Limited-scope representation uniquely satisfies the needs and wants of all because it allows everyone involved to decide together in advance of representation specifically what work will be performed by the lawyer for the client at a mutually agreeable cost to be paid (often in advance) by the client to the lawyer. As described by our Canadian friend and colleague, Brian Galbraith, it's like going to the auto sales lot and choosing between the base model vehicle, the fully loaded version with all the bells and whistles, or something in between with all options being priced accordingly.

In just a few short years, TLS grew from two attorneys with no staff to five attorneys with three staff, and the firm is well positioned to grow considerably more. TLS team members are chosen specifically for their shared dedication to building something better. TLS has been featured in multiple professional publications in Iowa and elsewhere. We have spoken at international events and worked with various local, national, and international groups. TLS now serves clients and colleagues through both our cutting-edge law practice and through teaching, coaching, and consulting services. Notably, although TLS started out by unbundling primarily in family law matters, perhaps the most complex area of practice for limited-scope work, we have found that unbundled concepts apply often and easily in many other areas of practice within our firm as well. Spreading understanding and use of unbundled legal services leads to better outcomes for consumers and their families, which in turn creates an overall societal benefit.

Using unbundled legal services combined with maximum firm efficiency processes, we have mindfully developed a law firm that is now a beacon of light for stressed out litigants and lawyers alike. For us, the design thinking process was more cyclical than linear. It wasn't a straight path to a successful firm model. We saw a need that included relief for our clients and ourselves. We noodled ideas for addressing that need and strung those ideas together in a way we felt made sense for everyone. We continue to hone and develop our ideas, our craft, and our mission. TLS is ever evolving, just as any business should be. Unbundled legal services make so much more possible than anything we experienced in a traditional law firm. With sufficient and continuing assessment and planning of our internal processes, we have less stress and we are able to genuinely enjoy our work on a daily basis. We can clearly envision a reasonable vacation, sabbatical, or even gradual exit strategy from the practice of law whenever we choose. We are helping people. We have happy clients and a wonderfully positive firm team. Carpe diem!

8

Applying the Steps: Reimagine the Client Journey in Litigation

Ginevra Saylor

On the heels of my one-year anniversary as Director, Innovation & Knowledge Programs with global law firm Gowling WLG's Canada region, I found myself in an enviable position. One of our practice groups sought help evaluating their processes, giving me the opportunity to suggest and ultimately engage them in a full-scale legal design thinking project. In 20+ years of working in law firm knowledge management and innovation, I had become a confirmed process re-engineering and legal design thinking evangelist. But with lawyers being a somewhat skeptical bunch and design thinking a relatively novel concept for law firms, initiating these projects tends to be a hard sell. I was delighted to discover a ready, willing, and very keen practice group on the doorstep. And so began our journey. The following describes why the firm invested in the project, how we designed and implemented it, and what we have learned from the experience so far.

Building the Case

The particular opportunity surfaced many months after a flourishing boutique firm in one of Gowling WLG's eight Canada region office locations combined with and became part of Gowling WLG. In the midst of integrating new technologies, operations, and processes, the former boutique's formidable litigation practice saw the merger as a perfect time for evaluating its approach to litigating matters to streamline processes, deliver greater value, and enhance overall client satisfaction. Nothing was broken; they were just looking for possible ways to take their game up a notch.

When the firm's Innovation Partner—located in the same local office—referred this litigation group to Innovation & Knowledge Programs for ideas, we recommended a legal design thinking project. The practice group members would need to commit considerable time to attending a series of workshops to map their clients' journeys from the moment they call the firm with a new case all the way through that matter's conclusion. The group would need to identify every step in their current approach to handling litigation, seeing it from their clients' perspective to discern what their clients are thinking, experiencing, and feeling. At the same time, the group would look for ways to fill gaps, tighten the process, and enhance the journey by crafting a future-state map. The litigation group welcomed the challenge and so we set about making the business case.

As with any project, the firm would need to understand the benefits and associated costs before committing to it. While the project would incur no hard costs, doing it well would demand a major investment of time and carry a notable opportunity cost. We estimated needing a minimum of 15 hours from at least two partners and two to four associates, as well as the same amount of time from a like number of law clerks and legal assistants. The project would also claim roughly five hours from the firm's Innovation Partner and anywhere from 30 to 50 hours from the Innovation & Knowledge Program director and team. This estimate covered only the project's design phase of mapping current and future states; implementing the future state would be another story.

Fortunately, with top leadership support from the local office's Litigation Practice Group Lead—who in fact fully backed the project—and the firm's Innovation Steering Committee—which counted among its members the firm's COO and Innovation Partner—the project was approved and the investment in time endorsed wholeheartedly. To compensate fee earners for time devoted to innovation projects, the firm had created a "fund" of hours; for compensation purposes, these hours count toward fee earners' billable-hours targets exactly as hours billed on client work. After earmarking a substantial number of hours from the fund for this project, we were ready to begin.

Building the Team

After drafting a project charter outlining the benefits, scope, assumptions, risks, milestones, deliverables, and other common components, the first big step was convening a full project team and roster of participants. Here, the first critical decision was whether to include our clients in the workshops. Because design thinking is all about the customer—or, in our case, client—experience, with the goal of designing to delight, you would think that ideally the customer would participate. After all, who better to supply the customer voice than the customer?

Yet, including clients is not always feasible or even preferred. In this project, we decided to involve only internal people in the current- and future-state mapping workshops for several reasons, three of which stand out. First, we recognized that this was likely to be a new experience for many (if not all) of our participating firm members, and so we might have greater likelihood of engendering open, frank, and unrestrained conversation if we kept the workshops internal. Second, we knew we already held a wealth of proxy data on our clients' experiences from client satisfaction interviews and surveys, end of matter discussions, and impromptu, informal feedback. Third, we recognized that most of our clients would likely be too busy and reluctant to contribute the amount of time needed to map the full litigation process in detail. The plan was to involve some key clients in later phases of the project.

Success in design thinking projects depends heavily on having one or two strong workshop facilitators who understand their role and know what they must both do and refrain from doing during the workshops. The facilitators' role is to spark discussion by asking questions that draw out each step and get the participants to describe who does what to complete each task and ensures all components of the map are documented before advancing to the next. Good facilitators keep discussions moving, prevent tangents, and respectfully enforce the ground rules. At this stage, facilitators need to avoid supplying answers and suggesting solutions—a natural temptation that can be hard to resist.

Another critical role is the project champion; this should be someone in a leadership position, who is highly respected and trusted, and can lend credibility to the process. We were fortunate to have as our champion the firm's Innovation Partner, a long-standing Gowling practitioner and former office Managing Partner with a far-reaching reputation for legal innovation and practice transformation. Including our champion in the first three-hour workshop built trust and goodwill and gave the project the needed gravitas.

Last and most importantly, we needed a representative and sufficient number of practice group members to ensure we would capture accurately all parts of the process, including points of intersection, gaps in flow, redundancies, and potential obstacles. Our participants included the office Litigation Practice Group lead and another partner, as well as junior and senior associates, law clerks, and legal administrative assistants; each of these roles contributes something different and each perspective is paramount to paint the full picture. All participants committed to attend a series of four three-hour workshops over the course of the next few months.

Charting the Journey

Eager to start, we shared our methodology with the participants, the core of which would be four workshops. Using flip charts, multicolor markers, and sticky notes of various sizes and color, the group would detail every step in the current litigation process, including:

- All tasks and interactions required to complete them;
- The clients' likely thoughts, feelings, and emotions at each point;
- Any potential issues and challenges; and
- Opportunities to enhance the client experience that might come to mind—although this would not be the main focus.

The facilitators would record and incorporate all of this into an evolving digital process map to share with the group for feedback in between sessions, and add any comments or additions received into the map before the next session. After completing the current-state map, the next step would be to brainstorm ideas and work together to build out a future-state map that closes gaps, streamlines processes, and most importantly smooths out any bumps and roadblocks in the client journey.

Finally, the future state process would be tested in a pilot and, with adjustments based on feedback from both litigation group members and clients, be implemented in that office. The end goal would be to replicate the pilot and implementation office-by-office, fine-tuning incrementally along the way, to embed a new firm-wide litigation process and practice of continuous improvement.

Design Thinking in Practice

We started our first workshop in February 2020 with a 60-minute, whirlwind crash course on process improvement, with a focus on understanding value from the client's perspective and eliminating waste. Some key concepts that we covered and returned to throughout the first and later workshops included the following:

- Empathizing with the client by answering probing questions like, "what causes frustration," "what feels harder than it should," and "what would make this easier" at each step in the process
- Understanding that clients see value as getting what matters most to them, and not paying for things that do not matter to them
- Identifying and eliminating actions that neither add nor enable value to the client as waste
- Looking for the common examples of waste in legal work, like doing more than clients want, taking too long to complete tasks, neither leveraging others' skills nor empowering them to act, poor feedback loops resulting in frequent requests for status updates, and unnecessarily moving people or materials

The first workshop was very successful. We were eager to schedule the next workshop for late March 2020 only to find ourselves in the midst of a pandemic and lockdown that—as we now know all too well—resulted in an unprecedented rapid pivot to remote working, which continues through the time of this writing.

Faced with a tough decision and very real risk of losing our momentum, we decided to try forging ahead by conducting the remaining workshops virtually over Zoom, simulating the same approach with virtual sticky notes on a virtual flip chart. We were genuinely surprised and relieved to find that these sessions were every bit as engaging and productive. In fact, the virtual workshops even offered some advantages, including the participants being more relaxed in their homes (not to mention comfortable clothing) and experiencing fewer interruptions (from people poking their heads into the conference room with a quick question or a document to be signed). Granted, we had on our side the established excellent rapport and rhythm developed through the first workshop; getting people comfortable speaking up without the benefit of that first in-person session undoubtedly would have been substantially harder.

On completing the workshops and process mapping, we faced a second major challenge. Before the pandemic and lockdown, the firm had started migrating from its long-standing document management system to a newer, cloud-based system. After a suspension of several months, the firm resumed the migration despite the continued lockdown and remote working. This naturally diverted attention from the design thinking project—as people needed to learn and become adept with a new core system—and has delayed piloting and implementing the future-state process. At the time of writing, we are enthusiastically picking up where we had stalled.

Lessons Learned

Every project is an opportunity to learn. This project was no different, with its share of things that went gratifyingly well and others not so well (which we will chalk up to experience). On reflection, what have we taken from this project?

On the positive side, both the overall methodology and format of the workshops worked as planned, even with the unanticipated lockdown. Although in-person workshops remain preferable, we learned that virtual settings can work—something worth knowing for global organizations that cannot always get people physically together in one place. The important lesson is to remain open-minded and flexible.

We also learned that having a highly motivated and keen group, interested in taking on a project of this magnitude and remaining dedicated throughout, is critical to success. Similarly, involving people in all roles and at all levels (assistants, law clerks, associates, and partners) is an absolute must; we never could have captured every task and step, nor teased out potential for client frustration or uncertainty at certain points, without the benefit of the unique perspective each person brought to the exercise. Finally, a strong and well-respected champion to set the stage and the local Practice Group lead's active participation in all of the workshops were instrumental in both securing committed participants and keeping them engaged throughout the lengthy project.

On the "chalk it up to experience side," being able to schedule the workshops closer together, as in a week instead of months apart, would have given the mapping process greater continuity. The more time that passed between sessions, the longer it took us to bring our collective thinking back to where we had stopped in the process and what we had revealed to that point. Another challenge is keeping minds fresh, focussed, and relaxed when everyone involved is extremely busy, pulled in many different directions, and likely drawn into a more pressing and stressful matter at any moment. In the future, we also plan to involve clients with whom we have a long and trusted relationship in the exercise of both mapping the client journey and envisioning an optimal future state.

9

Applying the Steps: Immigration Law

Greg Siskind

I never knew the term "design thinking" until just a few years ago when I attended a legal technology conference and there was a session on the subject led by well-known Vanderbilt law professor Cat Moon. Honestly, I attended the session because Cat always offers helpful insight, even though I had no idea what the panel would be about. What I heard made me realize that I had been incorporating design thinking into my practice for decades and never knew there was a whole body of knowledge on the subject.

My path in my career has largely been about finding novel solutions to problems rather than moving along the conventional path. I ended up finishing college in two and a half years when I was 19 because I was paying my own way and figured out that combining AP credits, 18-hour course loads, and discounted summer classes (along with eating a lot of ramen noodles and working two or three jobs at a time) meant I could finish faster and with little debt.

I graduated law school in 1990 and in the four years between receiving my JD and starting my own immigration law practice, I worked at a large law firm in Nashville. I was largely doing corporate law and, although the people at the firm were great and the work was challenging, it didn't take long for me to realize that this was not the life for me. For one, after handling my first immigration matter, I was hooked and wanted to switch to that field. My firm made it clear to me that this was not an option, my fiancée (now wife of 27 years) told me leaving the city wasn't an option, and there were no jobs available in the tiny immigration bar in a city that at the time didn't have a lot of immigration work. And I had very little capital, no reserves or family investors, and my new wife. I also had no clients or experience. So starting this venture was going to be a challenge.

But I did at least have ideas for new ways to run a practice that were more client-centric than had been tried in the past. One of the reasons I was able to survive those early years is because I got interested in the internet before most people and realized that one way to give people confidence in your ability as a lawyer—to demonstrate your expertise—could be shown through various internet platforms.

Starting in the early 1990s, in the days before the web, I began posting information on immigration law on early message boards called USENET newsgroups. The newsgroups on immigration—like most—were noncommercial, and "netiquette" required one to refrain from posting advertisements and solicitations. That was not a problem, because I was posting informational articles and answering general questions (with disclaimers, of course).

In 1993, the Mosaic graphical web browser was released and it presented a completely new, more friendly way to access information on the internet. Given that immigration law is a federal practice area and petitions were (and still are) filed by mail to regional offices, I bet that the web would be an engaging and easily accessible way to engage with potential clients.

From Idea to Prototype

I decided to launch a law firm and one of the first ever law firm websites simultaneously. The focus would be on universities and high-tech employers, because those are the places that had internet access at the time. The emphasis would be on providing in-depth content covering the latest developments in immigration law as well as introductory articles on immigration law. I would also make my website "sticky" by launching the first emailed law firm newsletter.

The law firm and the site www.visalaw.com[1] launched in June 1994 and although two other large firms in DC went online before me, a solo immigration law firm in Tennessee was a more interesting media story, and I got a lot of free publicity. Plus, it wasn't that hard to find my website if you were online and looking. There was no Google or other search engines. Just directories that were basically the web's table of contents. The site had massive traffic in those early days—millions of hits—because people were desperate for information on the U.S. immigration process and there just were no easy places to find it. I basically had two years with virtually no competition and in the first ten years, only a few lawyers[2] were presenting serious competition.

Aside from providing content on a website, the firm was built as a hybrid practice that offered services locally and virtually. Clients out of town booked appointments for phone consultations, we communicated with them by email, they uploaded documents to us via File Transfer Protocol or emailed them to us, and we emailed documents for review and signature. These are all unremarkable today, but at the time, we were just collaborating with clients to figure out ways to use the new technology to deliver our services in a better way.

Using Empathy to Identify Problems to Solve

Fast forward two decades and today we are still taking the same approach to delivering legal services, but using, for example, artificial intelligence-based expert systems to address pain points for our clients. What are the problems that are difficult to solve because they're too expensive to hire lawyers, there is not enough time, and lawyers are generally considered obstacles rather than facilitators? When lawyers are honed in on understanding the client's point of view, they often will discover ways to design their legal services that the client might not even know to ask for. I'm reminded of this quote, often and possibly erroneously attributed to Steve Jobs:

1. It helped that domain names were basically all still available when I selected ours in 1993. The prescient immigration lawyer Rajiv Khanna had already purchased immigration.com.

2. Carl Shusterman, Sheela Murthy, and Rajiv Khanna come to mind.

> Some people say, "Give the customers what they want." But that's not my approach. Our job is to figure out what they're going to want before they do. I think Henry Ford once said, "If I'd asked customers what they wanted, they would have told me, 'A faster horse!'" People don't know what they want until you show it to them. That's why I never rely on market research. Our task is to read things that are not yet on the page.

I don't agree that there's no place for market research. But rather than focusing on asking people to define what they need, you can focus on understanding their frustrations. In the Henry Ford example in Jobs' quote, the frustration was with slow transportation and people assumed they needed a faster horse. Ford understood how innovation could address this even if people didn't yet understand the technology.

That's the approach we're still taking today. A few case examples help to illustrate.

Testing and Refining New Solutions

Consultbot

An immigration lawyer typically needs an hour or more in an initial consultation with a client in order to assess their circumstances and recommend a strategy to meet their immigration needs. The first part of the consultation is focused on information gathering so that the lawyer can screen in and screen out options to be discussed in the second part of the meeting.

Lawyers have devised various methods to try and make the consultation more efficient. That might include having a paralegal interview the prospective client first. The risk of this is that the paralegal will fail to pick up on or understand key points. And this takes the paralegal away from work they otherwise might be working on, which can slow the turnaround of other clients' work. Some simply have the client complete an intake form and the lawyer can refer to that in a consultation. Unfortunately, without knowing anything about the case, the lawyer will either ask too many screening questions and waste the client's time or ask too few and still end up having to largely ignore the form because it doesn't provide enough useful information. In either scenario (or the more common one of a consultation simply taking place without any advance screening), the client isn't well served because their time is wasted or they're not getting the best advice from a lawyer who has missed issues because of poor screening.

A solution we have developed is the deployment of a chatbot that is for people who have already scheduled a time to speak to one of our lawyers. Chatbots are hardly new, but the way we're using this one is. The bot (and a soon to be employed web-based guided interview) take the client through a question set that has a pool of more than 500 potential questions, but will typically ask a tiny fraction according to defined question paths. The interviews are different for each person based on the programmed flow charts deployed in the interview. The end result is a transcript the lawyers can review as a quick reference to decide what to discuss. The next phase of the project will go a significant step further. Based on the bot interview, the app will make strategy recommendations and flag issues of concern.

The fully developed application will address a number of problems plaguing both lawyers and clients. First, clients can convey relevant information much more efficiently. Irrelevant questions are largely screened out. Questions can be programmed in multiple languages (with the report for the lawyer being delivered in English).

The consultation with the lawyer will be shorter and the lawyer will likely choose a better strategy. The odds of malpractice go down because the bot doesn't have biases and doesn't forget to ask questions or make faulty assumptions based on biases. The bot also will help as a training tool for newer lawyers who will get the benefit of more experienced lawyers who have helped develop the bot's logic and reporting.

H-1B Public Access File Generator

The H-1B visa is the visa available to people working in "specialty occupations" that require at least a bachelor's degree. It's used for medical doctors, computer programmers, school teachers, and various other professionals. As part of the application process, an employer must first file a Labor Condition Application (LCA) online with the U.S. Department of Labor (DOL) and then the H-1B application with U.S. Citizenship and Immigration Services (USCIS) after the DOL approves the LCA.

The filing of the LCA is normally handled by an immigration lawyer and then the filed LCA must be posted at the employer's worksite for several days and a "public access file" (PAF) must be created containing a variety of documents (including the filed LCA), which has to be available for inspection whenever anyone requests it (including government officials). The file must be created within 24 hours of the LCA being filed.

Most immigration lawyers pass the responsibility for preparing and maintaining this file to the client rather than actually preparing the PAF. Typically, the lawyer will send the filed LCA to the client and a memorandum telling them what needs to be in the PAF and the rules regarding compliance. There are a couple of reasons for this. First, the very short timeline for complying with the rule makes it very difficult logistically to get the PAF prepared in time. Second, the lawyer will typically need to charge extra for this service and clients have been reluctant to pay the added cost.

The problem is that clients have been lax about complying and the Department of Labor isn't interested in hearing excuses. In some cases, the work was delegated to a low-level employee and simply ignored. In others, the files were produced outside the time required or left out key items.

After enough discussions with clients about the compliance problems, we found a way to get to a solution that solves all of the problems—an expert system that makes it fast and easy to produce a compliant PAF that is timely. Our paralegal sends the submitted LCA copy along with an instruction email and a link to the client and they are taken to the PAF Generator app. They answer a series of relatively simple questions and upload requested documents. The PAF Generator produces a Public Access File with the required documents, posts online the required posting, sends the required notification via email to the foreign national, emails confirmation and a copy of the PAF (with a date stamp confirming timeliness) to those needing to ensure compliance (the lawyer, senior HR, in-house counsel, etc.). The whole process takes just a few minutes and we're able to ensure our clients are complying with the legal requirements in a timely manner, and can charge a fraction of what we would charge if we did the work directly. We have solved a long-standing headache for clients and created a new revenue stream since most clients wouldn't pay for us to do the work. And we are white labeling the software tool so our competitors can use the product too.

J-1 Physician Waiver Advisor

Our firm has a large physician immigration practice and we represent hospitals across the country. Foreign physicians constitute about a quarter of all the doctors in the United States and there is a serious doctor shortage in this country. In some fields (internal medicine, psychiatry), the percentage for foreign doctors is over 40 percent. Most international doctors are recruited from U.S. residency programs and state licensing rules generally require three-plus years of training by those with foreign medical degrees in U.S. teaching hospitals. Most of those international doctors enter the United States using a J-1 visa and they are required to depart the United States for two years following completion of their J-1 training.

Doctors can get a waiver of the home residence requirement, but this generally requires sponsorship by a U.S. government or state health agency. There are more than 55 of these programs, and the rules are different for each of them. Physician recruiters usually have to reach out to an immigration lawyer during the recruiting process to figure out if a doctor can be sponsored for a visa. Unfortunately, the rules are really complicated and there are a number of variables. Calling a lawyer before you can consider hiring someone is a big disincentive to spending energy on a potential candidate and a lot of recruiters simply avoid these doctors rather than reaching out to counsel. Lawyers can be slow in responding, they can be expensive and they can be intimidating to deal with. We decided many years ago to not charge for our time in reviewing a prospective physician candidate. The hope is that by removing the disincentive to reach out to us, we can increase the number of successful recruitments and grow our caseload accordingly. But it's time-consuming for us, and many clients still don't want to call a lawyer, free or not free.

So we developed a technology work-around. After years of developing logic for the dozens of different J-1 waiver programs (all hidden behind a simple interface), we have made it possible for recruiters to go through an interview and determine if a doctor is a likely approval or denial (or a maybe) for a J-1 waiver. After the interview, the recruiter gets a red, yellow, or green light; they know what the prospects are for recruiting the doctor. The answer comes instantaneously and the client also gets information on what information they will need to provide their lawyer. The recruitment process is sped up and the law firm gets the additional business (plus saves time we were having to eat because we couldn't charge for it without risking losing the higher paying work).

It also has the possibility of dramatically easing physician recruiting for rural hospitals and addressing that particular health care crisis.

There are endless possibilities for developing similar tools in our field that benefit both the client and the lawyer. The challenge is usually getting enough of a handle on the client experience to have a sense for what solutions clients need (whether they realize it or not).

10

Applying the Steps: Online Courses

Lisa Feldstein

Introduction

Online courses are wildly popular in virtually every industry, yet law is lagging behind. Certainly, as regulated professionals there are unique considerations. However, the field is ripe for innovation, and access to justice remains a problem. I believe with some thoughtful due diligence and a focus on simplicity, online courses can be a beautiful addition to legal practices that serve both users/clients and lawyers alike.

But first, who am I to be writing about online courses?

I am a health and fertility lawyer in Ontario, Canada. Since 2013, much of my practice has been focused on serving family caregivers. Like many lawyers with a niche, I've noticed patterns emerge. Some of my meetings with family caregivers started to feel like Groundhog Day. My heart would break when clients would say things like "I wish I found you sooner" or "I wish I had known that was an option." I knew I could help more people if only I could reach them.

Over time, as I gave the same advice over and over and over, I developed repeatable formulas that worked. I became more efficient and effective. I started to offer flat fees, with services backed by processes, systems, and automations.

I started to wonder if there would be a way I could "productize" my advice so that clients could pay a fraction of the price, while I also benefitted financially from the ability to scale. After all, the better lawyer I became, the less I was earning on the hourly model. And I have so much compassion for my clients I have been reluctant to raise my rates much.

Empathize

To determine what scale might look like (beyond hiring more lawyers), I began to ask clients how and where they looked for information when researching their legal problems. I also read reports created by caregiver think tanks. I learned that, not surprisingly, a lot of people perform research online. I started to join caregiver groups on Facebook to see what people were asking when I wasn't present, and what advice they received from their communities (spoiler alert: while there was a lot of wonderful social support, there was also *a lot* of inaccurate legal advice).

We began to call up past leads and clients to perform interviews. We asked questions such as:

- Where have you looked to find information about navigating the mental health system?
- What problems, if any, have you faced seeking information about how to help your loved one?
- What medium do you find the most useful to consume information (especially about complicated topics like law)? In other words, how do you prefer to learn new information?
- *If Applicable*—You called us to seek legal advice but didn't end up working with us. Why is that? Where else did you look? Did you find what you were looking for?
- We know that caregivers need a lot of support and resources. What kinds of supports or resources do you think a law firm could offer that would genuinely improve your life?

We recorded answers in a spreadsheet. Admittedly this was a messy approach. Long-winded answers are valuable, but are not easily contained in predefined boxes. We did it anyway, as best as we could. We performed phone interviews rather than sending out a written survey. This allowed us to ask follow-up questions and get a deeper understanding of the clients' challenges finding answers and support.

We also started to ask certain clients questions during our meetings, such as "How did you find that out? Where else did you look?"

Here are examples of some of the actual answers either I, my associate, or a law student recorded in response to our phone surveys:

- "She used online resources #1. She used CAMH [psychiatric hospital] website. She had a mental health advocate. Those were only two resources localized to Toronto. Mostly articles, some videos. She would have preferred video. It was one way consuming info, and then one on one conversations with people. When you're really stressed, sometimes reading is hard, so video easier."
- "We've been to the cops, Children's Aid Society, psychiatrist, family doctor, hospitals, everybody, justice of the peace (JOP). Last resort was JOP. JOP told her 'clearly system is broken.'"
- "Looked all over the internet, looked at every publication, talking to other people. The medical system doesn't get it, doctors don't understand, they sign the forms, but they give incorrect information."
- "Almost like Coles notes of information, that he might be able to click and view, he obviously would pay for it, education about what the proper laws are. Address things such as: What do you have to do, to get treated like a normal person, as family member of the patient? Their rights? Would like information about, can you challenge doctors? Can you say anything?"

As you can see, it is messy. It is shorthand that was captured while trying to have a live conversation. In hindsight, a notetaker or recording device would have been useful. But it nonetheless contained useful nuggets of information.

As we performed our research, we began to confirm that internet searches left a lot of people wanting more. We also confirmed that caregivers are often searching for information in panic mode, sometimes late at night. They need answers quickly. They need plain language and clear direction because stress makes it harder to process information.

Define (the Problem)

There are not many resources for family caregivers to learn about mental health law in Ontario, Canada. Some clients happen to have a family connection to a nurse or physician and they receive some pointers. Others encounter a supportive and knowledgeable social worker. But it is very piecemeal and not all-encompassing. The average person's research findings are not particularly useful, accurate, or strategic. There is a patchwork of information, sometimes from the wrong jurisdiction, that is cobbled together in a frenzy.

In many ways, this was not a new finding. After all, I had been serving family caregivers since 2013. What was new was the lightbulb that began glowing above my head that was trying to light the way forward. I just wasn't sure which direction to go.

Ideate

Before interviewing clients, I admittedly had already started to imagine what a different service model might look like. I knew some clients would always want or need one-to-one services. But might some be able to achieve the same outcome with automated guidance? An app? Access to a digital library? Webinars? Membership?

After speaking with past clients and leads, I began thinking about other models that might meet their needs: a peer support network, a conflict resolution service, or an interdisciplinary platform that incorporated guidance from health professionals. Even after launching online courses, we are continuing to advance some of the other ideas that emerged from our research.

I ultimately settled on online courses because it matched a lot of the gaps identified in our interviews. Courses could be created with a combination of video and text to match various learning styles. The content could be accessed by users immediately. Courses could be updated easily if the law changed. And they could be worked on at my own pace.

Looking back, I admit I first fell into a trap of trying to do too much at once. I actually wanted to create courses and a membership all in one. I spent months and months testing software but could not find anything that met my needs. I fell victim to perfectionism. I learned an important lesson: keep it simple. It's wonderful to have a vision of your finished product, but that is an unrealistic goal for the first version and can actually hinder your progress.

Prototype

Before creating my courses I spoke with a few other lawyers who had already done so. One told me he made beautiful, detailed, high-value courses and that not too many people bought them. He said he would often give them away for free to clients, but did not earn much money on them. That was a cautionary tale I took to heart. I decided to create relatively simple courses.

After testing a lot of the course-building software I ended up choosing one that had the most generous free trial because I knew I would be creating it on and off in my "spare time." In the end, I chose software that was far simpler than its competitors. One day I might switch, but for now I find value in its simplicity. With simple software there are few things to tinker with, fewer distractions. I post new lessons quickly and move on.

The first course we launched wasn't particularly well organized or thought out. I mapped out a few lessons, but mostly created the course directly in the software. I wouldn't recommend this approach as I think it is prudent to have a backup of the material, which will also be useful if you decide to switch platforms. Live and learn. Next time I will start in Word. I recommend you begin your course-building journey there as well.

I also started with text and just a few videos. I did not edit my videos, or add effects or music, although that would have enhanced the quality. I used Loom (the free version), and then uploaded videos that are all five minutes or less. I have taken several online courses that are beautifully designed and the effort behind them is extraordinary. However, I decided not to create that level of visual quality for my first course and I have no regrets. At this point I was just building the most basic version of what my course could be—focused on the legal substance and not much else. This is consistent with the advice I've learned elsewhere about building products, whether digital or not. The "minimum viable product" (MVP) is enough at this early stage.

I have spent a fair bit of time learning from industry experts about courses, memberships, and other ways to transform my legal practice into a scalable modern business. And I've learned that overwhelm is a common problem. It is easy to want to provide an abundance of information, but too much can be paralyzing for the recipient. It is better to have short bite-sized lessons that allow people to make progress and gain momentum in small chunks of time. This takes discipline because as lawyers we want to share every exception and nuance. But we can actually help people get results and digest information in a course by simplifying and narrowing what we offer. You might actually be making a course higher in value by exercising restraint.

Test

Seek Feedback

When we launched our first course, we didn't announce it to the world. Instead, we provided free access to friends and family over a period of several months. Sure, they weren't exactly the avatar, but they were a group of people who cared enough to read through the material and catch any glaring errors before we shared it with clients.

When people called our firm asking about our services I would assess whether they were a good fit for the course. We were transparent that the course was brand new, and we expressed enthusiasm around them enrolling in the DIY option rather than retaining us. After all, it would save some folks a lot of money. By mentioning that the course was new we managed expectations and invited people to send us feedback along the way. We also have an optional survey at the end of the course.

Marketing Matters

Just because you build it does not mean they will come (at least not in droves). I did not plan a grand launch, and I did not have a grand opening. People signed up in trickles. This further validated that it is just fine to release a basic course and make it better over time. After launching my three evergreen courses I continue to refine them.

Additionally, one of my courses is a DIY version of a service we offer. Many clients are choosing to hire us over buying the course because they want the hand-holding and the ability to have someone else do the majority of the work. I made an error in thinking what people want most is a low price, forgetting that people will pay for speed and peace of mind.

I have no regrets about making the DIY course as it advances access to justice, and I believe it is acting as a signal of my authority as a subject matter expert (leading to more files in the area). However, it reinforces the importance of keeping it simple and confirming whether your course is even something the market wants.

Three Approaches

There is no one-size-fits all approach to courses, and every lawyer will have to take into account the applicable ethical duties. But here are some ideas of ways courses might fit into your practice.

1. Your course could be designed to prepare your clients *before* retaining your services.

Some people will always want or need one-on-one legal services. But a course can be used to educate clients *before* you even meet them. For example, a course on partnership agreements could help clients educate themselves about what decisions need to be made. Or whether to use a partnership versus corporation. If they decide they want to enter a partnership, they will know how to reach you and already have a clear idea of what terms they want in their contract. A course on patents could help potential clients understand what they need to do at the early stages to protect their inventions when they can't afford a lawyer but can afford—and truly need—a little guidance.

Can you develop a course that grooms or vets your leads? Can you develop a course, whether paid or free, that ensures your experience working with the client will be more productive? Can a course be a free lead magnet that you promote in your marketing?

A course can feel overwhelming and, for that reason, it may be more manageable to start in baby steps. Perhaps you have an infographic that maps out your process at a high level. Or a list of questions. Or a worksheet. Or tips. Or a checklist. Whatever it is, you can start with one thing at a time. You can use these to test your concept and see if there is an audience for that kind of resource.

2. Your course could be designed to support your clients *after* retaining your services.

Not all courses have to be a substitute for legal services. Courses can be sold to clients as a way to continue their education after a service is rendered. After drafting employment contracts, an employment lawyer could upsell an employer who wants to continue becoming familiar with the various employment laws; every week or month could cover a new topic (this might also work as a membership). A divorce lawyer could provide ongoing education to clients so they are constantly being mindful of legal landmines that are tied to events on the calendar such as Christmas and back-to-school. You could also create courses as a value-add to flat fee services or limited scope engagements.

A corporate lawyer might be able to create a simple DIY course on registering a trade name (depending on the jurisdiction).

A lawyer who serves entrepreneurs could create a training series for new business owners. Whenever a person signs up for the course they could start at the beginning, and lessons could be released or "dripped" out over time. The course could even be used as a marketing tool and contain upsells for contracts or other advice the business owner might need at various stages.

3. Your course could be *in lieu* of traditional legal services.

Do you have a service that can be broken down into steps and explained clearly to others? If so, it might be the seed of your first course. If you have checklists and templates that can guide people on how to go through a process, each step could become a lesson. Your process could be transformed into a product that is sold many times over. This is the epitome of "work hard once." Depending on the software, you could time lessons to appear at different intervals or to be available immediately.

Through our research I learned that caregivers need on-demand information to address the crisis before them, and I didn't want to make them wait for lessons to be released over time. One of our courses is designed to achieve a particular result; another is to provide support to caregivers who have a loved one going through a particular type of hearing; and the third course is to provide general education to caregivers who are beginning to navigate the mental health system. Each course has a different, but clearly defined, purpose.

People who sign up for the courses are *not* clients. This is stated in our FAQs and the disclaimer. They do not provide us with or upload any information about their case. They do not have to go through any intake process and can simply dive into the material.

In all of our courses we offer a few free lessons so users can confirm whether the course is right for them. This helps reduce the risk of an unhappy customer who bought a course they did not want or need.

As mentioned earlier, one of my courses parallels a service that we offer. When people contact our office we let them know that they are a good candidate for the course and can save a lot of money going the DIY route—yet, most of those folks have decided to pay more money for the benefit of our personalized guidance. As a result, I plan to offer one of our courses as a live program for clients over a six-week period. Clients will have access to the content, as well as live webinars and an opportunity to ask me questions. I will charge this at a higher price than the DIY course, but lower than the one-on-one service due to the economies of scale. I call this model "group legal coaching" and am working toward ways to add more of this into my practice (which, admittedly, is a slow and challenging process due to the many ethical and professional considerations). I have spoken with my insurance company, regulatory body, and lawyers in various jurisdictions who are pursuing innovative approaches to their practices. While progress may at times be slow, I am always moving forward. I hope you'll join me.

11

Applying the Steps: Wills and Estate Planning Software

Jordan M. Atin

The Problem: A Dated, Lawyer-Centric Process

I am just a will-drafting lawyer. Funny thing is that the process for preparing wills hasn't changed much over the past few hundred years. The only thing that has really changed is the use of a word processor. The will planning lawyer and the client have always sat across the desk from one another and just talked. Nothing but words were utilized to explain concepts, track instructions, or show implications of decisions. Private notes were kept by the lawyer. The client didn't know if what they were saying was being properly understood and the lawyer didn't know if the client was understanding the advice being given. Lastly, there was no real structure given to the meeting. It was free form and often scattered. Issues that came up would be addressed, but often those issues were only flagged because the lawyer remembered to do so.

Empathy Sparks an Idea

I had used that same process for the first ten years of practice. I don't know exactly what made me change, but I decided to keep track of those concepts and instructions on a whiteboard in front of the client. I often wondered whether during our meeting my client and I were on the same page so I decided to use the whiteboard as our common page. At first it was just keeping track of information for both the client and me. I would list the client's assets and write out the instructions on the disposition of assets and the choice of executors. At that point, I still didn't have any framework or structure for guiding clients through the complexities.

Over time I started to think of an easier way for clients to think about planning their wills. It started with breaking down the possibilities into a number of limited options. For example, rather than bouncing around from issue to issue or situation to situation, I discovered that in most cases, it can be broken down into three simple factual situations:

1. What do you want to do if you're the first to die, but your spouse is still alive?
2. What do you want to do if both you and your spouse are dead, but you have children or other descendants alive?
3. What do you want to do if everyone is gone?

Those scenarios were easy to understand and think through, but more importantly allowed us to focus on one situation at a time.

I was also trying to come up with a way to explain all the different options a client has for making gifts, gifts with no strings, gifts with conditions, trusts, and so on.

I recognized as a lawyer that there were so many different options, but that would be overwhelming for the client and I might lose them. I decided to break it down into only two gift options that would cover every kind of gift. Was there a "but" attached to the gift? If no, the proposed gift was "absolute"—no strings attached. If the client described the gift using the word "but" ("however" and "if" both count!), they were asking for a "trust" gift. Clients picked up on that immediately. It was an easy way to explain it and understand it.

With that, I had my methodology—the "3/2" framework. I started to use that on my whiteboard, and my iPhone was full of pictures of whiteboards with three scenarios and two types of gifts. Although I didn't realize it at the time, this was the genesis of eState Planner.

Testing, Refining, and Transforming

A friend of mine who had dealt with many estate planning lawyers for his clients over the years, loved the concept and suggested that I digitize it. In Starbucks across Toronto, I started to sketch out the visual approach that I used on my whiteboard. I thought about how I might use that on a screen where I could easily insert or delete gifts. I thought about how I could further break down the planning decisions. I decided to break down the transfer of gifts into one of three slots in the estate plan.

1. Gifts that flow outside of the will, such as life insurance designations and joint assets (what I call "Joint and Designated Assets")
2. Specific gifts off the top (what I named "Initial Gifts")
3. The balance of what was left over

Once that concept took shape I was able to design the layout of the software—three separate scenarios, two options for gifts, and three spaces where those gifts could be made.

I quickly realized that one of the great benefits was that the data that lawyers typically didn't use in any meaningful way—asset values—was now able to be leverage to show the impact of decisions in real amounts.

The software created a graphic representation of a client's will in real time. It became a collaborative and interactive experience between the client and me. Far better as a client experience than the words-only approach.

As a lark, I hired a small company to create the first version of eState Planner. It was clunky and didn't work very well. It didn't have many features but it was basically the whiteboard on a screen. I tried to use it myself and convince other lawyers to do so, but it didn't work well enough for any of us.

I was planning on abandoning it when my longtime colleague insisted that we re-do it from start and create a fully functioning version.

When reimagining the new version, I recognized that the great advantage that software has over the whiteboard is the ability to leverage the data and use it in many ways. On a whiteboard, the values and instructions were static. In software, that data could be used to provide red flags to the lawyer of important issues or inappropriate instructions. It could take all the data and fashion a comprehensive report letter and summaries. Lastly, rather than having to re-enter all the data that you collected from the client into a document, software could take all of that data and create a bespoke will taking into account all of the instructions without making technical mistakes.

It took another two years of development, but the next version had many of my dreamt of features: real-time calculations, good-looking graphics, reminders of legal issues that until then I had to remember myself, and the generation of very solid and comprehensive documents that could be generated not only for simple situations but also very complex ones as well.

In July 2019, it was ready to be launched to other lawyers. There were lots of issues and missing features. Lawyers like perfection and software is never perfect. A few lawyers joined up and we started to improve and add features. I found that many of the lawyers thought it made the will planning process too easy and that clients would feel that the lawyer wasn't really adding value. Those lawyers use it behind the scenes to ensure that they don't forget any issues, prepare summaries they can send to clients, and generate the documents. For me, I think that neglects the very reason that I created the software in the first place—a better client experience. I have learned that you can't convince everyone to change what they are used to, even when they would acknowledge it is a better method.

We went from ten firms in the first few months to 300 in under two years. The work never stops. We have a list of 300 features or enhancements we want to add and I doubt that the list will ever stop growing. Now that we have technology to enhance the will planning process, there's no going back.

PART IV

Design Worksheets for the Five Design Thinking Steps

Some of the worksheets in this section are available for download at http://ambar.org/design-your-practice-download.

12

Researching Your Clients' Needs Worksheet

This worksheet is designed to assist you as you work through the first step of the design thinking process (Empathize: Research Your Clients' Needs).

Step 1: Determine the method(s) you will use to collect client feedback. Examples include:

- One-on-one conversations
  - Pros: Can ask follow-up questions to drill down and really understand what the client needs.
  - Cons: More time-consuming than other options and could be difficult to get clients to set aside the time.
- Focus group(s)[1]
  - Pros: Can ask follow-up questions and the group setting could spur discussion among participants, which could lead to greater depth and understanding of client issues and needs.
  - Cons: More time-consuming than other options and could be difficult to get clients to set aside the time.

1. Unsure what a focus group is? Check out this description and guide: https://resources.pollfish.com/market-research/what-is-a-focus-group-and-how-to-use-it-in-your-market-research/#The%20Pros.

- Client survey
  - Pros: Less time-consuming for you and the client.
  - Cons: Can't ask follow-up questions in real time to better understand what the client needs.

Step 2: Ask the following questions:

- What works well for the client?
- What doesn't work well for the client?
- What changes could you make to improve the client's experience?

Step 3: Synthesize the data and make changes.

- What trends do you see?

  ____

  ____

  ____

- What changes can you make to your firm or what new services can you offer that are responsive to the client feedback shared and needs identified?

  ____

  ____

  ____

13

Defining the Problem Worksheet

This worksheet is designed to assist you as you work through the second step of the design thinking process (Define the Problem: A People-Centered Approach).

First, for your target client, write out your initial problem statement based on what you learned during step 1 of the design thinking process. As you craft it, ask yourself the following three questions:

1. What are your clients experiencing?
2. What is the legal issue?
3. What are their goals and needs?

____

____

____

Next, work through the four-step process outlined in Chapter 2.

Step 1: Humility. Be humble, check your biases.
Do you have any preset beliefs or expectations about how legal services are experienced? If yes, what are they?

____

____

____

How do your target clients experience legal problems?

____

____

____

Step 2: Listen and Learn. Ask why repeatedly until the "true" problem emerges.
Why [insert client problem here]?

Answer: ____

Why [insert answer from above]?

Answer: ____

Why [insert answer from above]?

Answer: ____

Why [insert answer from above]?

Answer: ____

Why [insert answer from above]?

Answer: ____

Step 3: Synthesize. Use the data and the insights you have gathered through listening and inquiry and build your problem statement using this template:

> **[Person/people who are the center of the problem statement in a descriptive way]. . .needs [use a verb]. . .because [your compelling insight].**

____

____

____

- Does the scope of this problem generate solution possibilities?
- Have you used compelling language?
- Is the focus of the problem on the client?

Step 4: Test and refine. Articulate four or five client personas, consider your problem statement from the perspective of each persona, and adjust/refine the problem statement as needed.

Present your problem definition to target clients and see what they say. Do they agree? Disagree? Do they have other thoughts?

Target client	Do they agree or disagree with your problem statement?	Other feedback shared	Changes to the problem statement

It's ideal to ask real people, but if that is not possible, you can also consider your problem statement against your different client personas.

Persona	Moti-vation	Needs	Emotions	Attributes	Possible reaction to getting a bill	Changes to problem statement

Based on the feedback you received, tweak your problem statement. Remember to use this template:

[Person/people who are the center of the problem statement in a descriptive way]. . .needs [use a verb]. . .because [your compelling insight].

____

____

____

14

Ideation Worksheet and Checklist

Lori Gonzalez

This worksheet is designed to assist you as you work through the third step of the design thinking process (Ideate—How to Solve the Problem)

Checklist

Innovation Space:

- Comfortable and inviting seating
- Food and beverages
- Location and parking accessible
- Wellness break areas

Innovation Team:

- Legal professionals
  - Attorneys
  - Billing clerks
  - Paralegals
  - Secretaries
  - Law students/law clerks
- Technologists

- Clients
- Legal adjacent vendors
- Industry professionals outside of legal
  - Accounting/banking
  - Manufacturing
  - Health care

Supply list:

- Whiteboard/large writing area
- Markers/pens/highlighters
- Post-it notes (all sizes)
- Tape
- Colored dots (for voting)

Ideation Worksheet

Problem statement ____

____

Consider the following:

- Who—Who are you building for?
- What—What is the desired outcome?
- When—When is the best time to launch?
- Where—Where will services be provided?
- How—How will the services be provided?

Play with the following concepts to generate your ideas:

Read/Write	Voice/E-communication
Style/Pattern	Process/Procedure
Space/Time	Color or Numeric Coding
Color/Graphics	Software/Systems
Learning/Teaching	Outsourcing/In-house
In-person/Virtual	Value Proposition
Points/Score	Education/Experience
Building/Re-creating	People/Automation
Fears/Misconceptions	Benefits/Features
Learning/Education	Management/Staff

Ideas:

15

Prototyping, Testing, and Refining Worksheet

Select the best idea you generated during the brainstorming process to pursue. What is the solution you'd like to test out and get feedback on?

____

____

____

Step 1: Define your "why" of prototyping.
Does your proposed solution involve technology?

- If yes, use a wireframe as your first prototype.
- If no, use a drawing on a piece of paper as your first prototype.

What feedback and knowledge are you looking to gain from building your wireframe or drawing and sharing it with target clients?

____

____

____

Step 2: Build your wireframe or create your drawing, share it with target clients, and collect feedback.

Target client	Did they under-stand the solution?	What did they like about the solution?	What did they dislike about the solution?	Did they find the solution valuable?	What tweaks can you make to improve the solution?

Synthesize the feedback, make the tweaks, and repeat this step until your feedback is mostly positive.

Step 3: Build a minimum viable product or service.
It's now time to take your prototype to the next level. What feedback are you looking to gain at this next stage?

___

___

___

- If your solution involves technology, decide if you are going to use an off-the-shelf product or build a custom solution.
- If your solution is a process change or service, can you build a slightly more advanced version of the solution that will help you obtain the feedback you are seeking?
- Will you do an alpha test or beta test? If the latter, will it be open or closed?
- Remember that you are not building the final product yet! You are simply seeking to build a prototype that helps you gain the feedback you outlined earlier.

Build the minimum viable product or service, conduct your test, and collect feedback.

Target client	**Did they understand the solution?**	**What did they like about the solution?**	**What did they dislike about the solution?**	**Did they find the solution valuable?**	**What tweaks can you make to improve the solution?**

Synthesize the feedback, make the tweaks, refine the solution, and repeat this step until your feedback is mostly positive.

Step 4: Continue to create more advanced prototypes, test, and refine until you have built a viable solution.

Step 5: Design a measurement and evaluation system.
How will you measure and evaluate whether your solution is solving the problem you defined?

____

____

____

16

Client Persona Worksheets

TIFFANY & JOHN WILLIAMS

NEW PARENTS - NEED A WILL

Age: 32 and 35
Location: Southwestern Chicago suburbs
Relationship Status: New parents
Income: Household income of $120,000+
Education: Bachelor's degrees
Work: Nurse and Customer Service Manager

CHALLENGES

They are overwhelmed with their new parental responsibilities. They're always questioning if they're "doing things right" with respect to their child. Not sure who they'd ask to take care of their child in case of an emergency.

WHAT THEY VALUE

- Convenience
- Trust
- Anything that will help them be the best parents they can be
- Affordability

COMMUNICATION

- Prefer to handle matters over the phone or via video chat
- Like posting pictures of their child on Instagram

THEIR GOALS

- Be the best parents they can be while also maintaining their full-time jobs, their marriage, etc.
- Start saving early for their child's future

VIEW OF LAWYERS

They have a few friends who have used them for divorces and closings with mixed reviews. No personal experience to date and no lawyers in their families.

RAMON CORTEZ

CHEF - SMALL BUSINESS STARTUP

Age: 37
Location: Downtown Denver
Relationship Status: In a relationship
Income: Has savings and is self-employed but not making any money yet
Education: Culinary degree
Work: Chef/Small Business Owner

CHALLENGES

Finding the capital to launch his business, finding an affordable location, and figuring out all of the things he needs to do to launch a successful business.

WHAT THEY VALUE

- Knowledge about the process
- Affordability
- Flexibility
- Hard work
- Saving time and money

COMMUNICATION

- Prefer to handle matters over the phone or via video chat
- Likes to text
- Works long days and needs flexible communication times

THEIR GOALS

- To open his restaurant within six months
- To have all of the "paperwork" out of the way before the launch

VIEW OF LAWYERS

Hasn't had any personal experience with them but has been told by other small business owners to consult one. He's not sure what he needs from a lawyer though.

____

____

Age: ______________________

Location: ______________________

Relationship Status: ______________

Income: ______________________

Education: ______________________

Work: ______________________

CHALLENGES

____

____

____

____

____

____

WHAT THEY VALUE

- ______________________
- ______________________
- ______________________
- ______________________

COMMUNICATION

- ______________________
- ______________________
- ______________________
- ______________________

THEIR GOALS

- ______________________
- ______________________
- ______________________
- ______________________

VIEW OF LAWYERS

____

____

____

____

____

17

Client Journey Map

Example

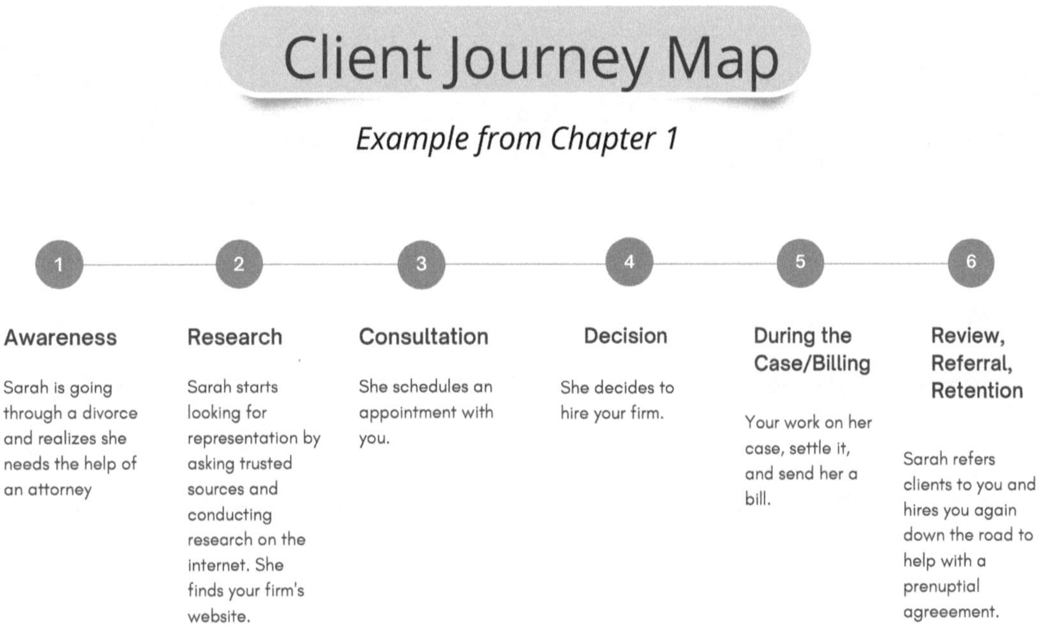

Template

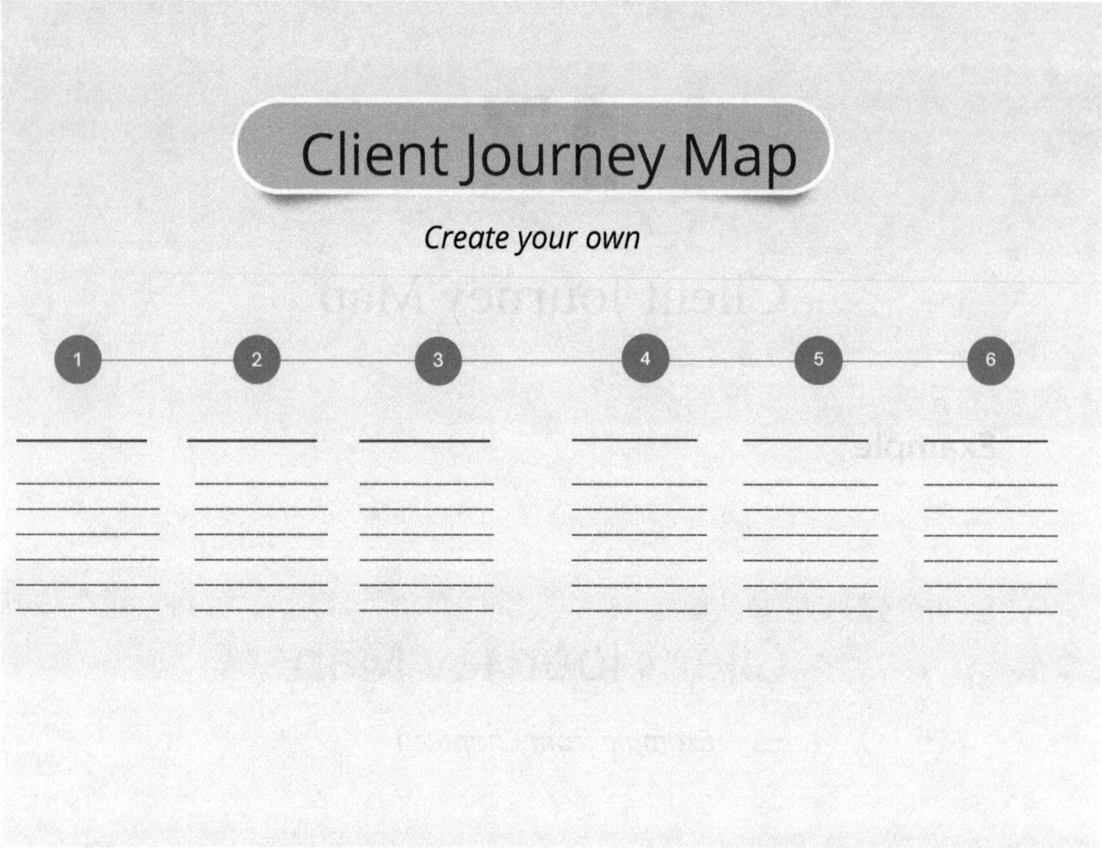

For Further Reading

Alice Armitage, Andrew K. Cordova & Rebecca Siegel, *Design-Thinking: The Answer to the Impasse between Innovation and Regulation*, Soc. Sci. Rsch. Network 2 (Aug. 23, 2017), https://papers.ssrn.com/sol3/papers.cfm?abstract_id=3024176.

Maria Camacho, *In Conversation: David Kelley: From Design to Design Thinking at Stanford and IDEO*, 2(1) She Ji: J. Design, Econ., & Innovation 88–101 (Spring 2016), https://researchbank.swinburne.edu.au/file/2aae1909-268b-4940-878e-68fffb83251d/1/pdf (published version).pdf.

Chicago Bar Foundation and A Different Practice, Pricing Toolkit (2021), https://chicagobarfoundation.org/resources/practice/pricing-toolkit/.

Veronique Fraser & Jean-François Roberge, *Legal Design Lawyering: Rebooting Legal Business Model with Design Thinking*, 16(2) Pepp. Disp. Resol. L.J. 303–16 (May 1, 2016), https://digitalcommons.pepperdine.edu/cgi/viewcontent.cgi?article=1359&context=drlj.

Jordan Furlong, Law Is a Buyer's Market: Building A Client-First Law Firm (2017) (ebook).

Kathrine Galloway & Nickolas James, Faculty of Law, Ctr. for Pro. Legal Educ., Presentation at Australasian Law Teachers Association Conference: A Critical Evaluation of the Relevance of Design Thinking for Lawyers (July 4–6, 2018), https://research.bond.edu.au/en/publications/a-critical-evaluation-of-the-relevance-of-design-thinking-for-law.

Margaret Hagan, Law by Design (2017), https://lawbydesign.co/.

IDEO, https://www.ideo.com/.

Lois R. Lupica, Tobias A. Franklin & Sage M. Friedman, *The Apps for Justice Project: Employing Design Thinking to Narrow the Access to Justice Gap*, XLIV Fordham Urb. L.J. 1363 (Dec. 14, 2017), https://papers.ssrn.com/sol3/papers.cfm?abstract_id=3086674.

Jack Newton, The Client Centered Law Firm (2020).

Stanford Legal Design Lab, Legal Design Toolbox, https://legaltechdesign.com/LegalDesignToolbox/.

Mark Szabo, *Design Thinking in Legal Practice Management*, 21(3) DMI Rev. 44–46 (Sept. 29, 2010), https://onlinelibrary.wiley.com/doi/abs/10.1111/j.1948-7169.2010.00078.x.

Susan Ursel, *Building Better Law: How Design Thinking Can Help Us Be Better Lawyers, Meet New Challenges, and Create the Future of Law*, 34(1) Windsor Y.B. Access to Just. 28–59 (Dec. 31, 2016), https://core.ac.uk/display/151777892.

About the Editors

Jessica Bednarz

Jessica Bednarz is the director of legal services and the profession at the Institute for the Advancement of the American Legal System (IAALS). In this role, Jessica is responsible for overseeing IAALS' work in the areas of the delivery of legal services and the legal profession and leading the vision and strategy of IAALS' work around innovation, reform, and evolution of the legal profession and its regulation, as well as the broader delivery of legal services. Prior to working at IAALS, Jessica was the associate director of innovation & the JEP for The Chicago Bar Foundation (CBF). In this role, Jessica was responsible for maintaining a culture of innovation at the CBF, directing special projects that advanced innovation in the practice of law, and overseeing all aspects of the Justice Entrepreneurs Project (JEP). The JEP helps lawyers launch socially conscious and innovative law practices targeting the underserved middle market. Jessica is also the co-founder of A Different Practice. Prior to working at the CBF, Jessica was in private practice specializing in family law, both as a solo practitioner and as an associate at O'Connor Family Law, P.C. Jessica earned a law degree from DePaul University College of Law, where she graduated cum laude and earned a Family Law Certificate, and a bachelor of science degree in business from Indiana University. Jessica resides in Denver, Colorado, and in her free time, enjoys exploring the outdoors, traveling, and community gardening.

Catherine Sanders Reach

Catherine Sanders Reach is director for the Center for Practice Management at the North Carolina Bar Association. Formerly she was director, Law Practice Management and Technology, for the Chicago Bar Association and the director at the American Bar Association's Legal Technology Resource Center. She is a frequent speaker and writer for bar associations and law schools. In 2011, she was selected to be one of the inaugural Fastcase 50, celebrating 50 innovators, techies, visionaries, and leaders in the field of law. In 2013, she was inducted as a fellow of the College of Law Practice Management. In 2015, she was selected to be part of the ABA LTRC Women of Legal Tech. She was co-chair of ABA TECHSHOW 2020.

Juda Strawczynski

Juda Strawczynski is a lawyer and frequent speaker and writer on legal services regulation and legal practice. He is the CEO and Registrar of the College of Patent Agents & Trademark Agents (CPATA), the independent public interest regulator of patent agents and trademark agents in Canada. He was previously the Director of practicePRO, LAWPRO's claims prevention and risk management initiative. Before joining LAWPRO, Juda was a policy counsel at the Law Society of Ontario, where he advised on key issues facing the legal professions, including access to justice, professional regulation, and consumer protection issues. Juda previously practiced at two litigation boutique law firms. He has also served as the volunteer president of Canadian Lawyers for International Human Rights, a fellow at Physicians for Human Rights, a law clerk at the Federal Court, and a director of the Canada Millennium Scholarship Foundation. Juda has a BA from McGill University and JD from the University of Toronto. He lives in Toronto, Canada.

About the Authors

Jess Birken

Jess Birken is the owner of Birken Law Office, helping nonprofits solve problems so they can quit worrying and get back to what matters most—The Work. She has a JD from Mitchell Hamline School of Law, an MA in nonprofit management, and is a certified transformative mediator. She worked her way through law school and had the beginnings of a promising career in criminal law after graduation. However, she quickly realized that going to court is depressing! In court, the toothpaste is out of the tube and you're just trying to clean up the mess. As a result, she went back to grad school and earned a master's in nonprofit management. She rejoined the nonprofit sector through her work with Pheasants Forever, where her role was a marriage of attorney work and federal grant management and administration. Since that time, she has run her own firms.

Jack Newton

As the CEO and founder of Clio and a pioneer in cloud-based legal technology, Jack Newton has spearheaded efforts to educate the legal community on the security, ethics, and privacy issues surrounding cloud computing, and has become a nationally recognized author and speaker on these topics. Jack has set a mission for himself and Clio to transform the practice of law, for good, and for more than a decade, his commitment has been unwavering. Jack's tremendous vision has already made a deep impact on one of the world's oldest professions. Jack is also the author of *The Client-Centered Law Firm,* which is helping law firms thrive in today's experience-driven era.

Sarah McCoubrey and Meredith Brown

Sarah McCoubrey and Meredith Brown are principals at CALIBRATE, a consultancy that delivers strategy, problem solving, and project management focused on increasing access to justice, protecting the rule of law, and improving service delivery to meet people's needs. Sarah has a bachelor's degree with a major in women's studies; a JD in law from UVic; and a master's of education in adult education, curriculum, and learning from OISE. Sarah has completed additional certifications in change management and collective impact frameworks.

Sarah practiced at Shibley Righton, LLP, in Toronto, focusing on education law, followed by ten years as the executive director of the Ontario Justice Education Network, combining her interests in law, education, and social justice. She received the Peter Cory Community Leadership Award for her efforts in justice education. She works on projects around the globe to build resilient justice systems that prioritize human rights and rule of law protections.

Meredith has a bachelor's degree with a Specialist designation in international relations and a JD in law. She spent 17 years with the Ministry of the Attorney General for Ontario as a labor and employment lawyer and in court administration to tackle the challenges facing that system. She served as chief legal counsel to three deputy attorneys general. She was the executive director of MAG's Innovation Office, introducing a culture of transformation and delivering successful change by working creatively with private sector, judicial, and community representatives. She leads evaluations and assessments on justice system functionality and performance, gender equality, human rights, and access to justice.

Lori Gonzalez

Lori Gonzalez is the CEO/Foundation at RayNa Corp. She has years of experience helping law firms improve their business and expand their services with technology and improvements to processes and procedures. She helps law firms test, implement, and train staff on legal tech and efficiency methods to improve growth and productivity. Lori is a frequent speaker at state and local bar associations, and presents at national conferences. As an access to justice advocate and legal tech enthusiast, she shares her knowledge with nonprofit organizations and committees that seek to advance the practice of law or improve access to justice through automation and tech solutions. She served on the Tennessee Access for Justice Commission's Pro Bono Committee, as an organizer of the Music City Legal Hackers, and as a creator of new tools for access to justice with Code for America's Nashville brigade. She served on the State Bar of California's Access Through Innovation of Legal Services Task Force and the advisory board for the University of Las Vegas—William S. Boyd School of Law's Tech and Innovation Initiative. She served on the 2022 ABA TechShow Board. Recent awards include recognition from Women of Legal Tech and ABA Legal Rebel.

Hersh Perlis

Hersh Perlis is the co-founder and director of the Legal Innovation Zone (LIZ) at Toronto Metropolitan University (TMU, formerly named Ryerson University). Since co-founding the LIZ, Hersh has helped grow it into a leader in the legal innovation space and has worked with law firms, corporations, and governments, nationally and internationally, to help identify and better prepare them to take advantage of the opportunities technology and other innovations present in today's ever-changing world. He has spoken extensively on the impact technology will have on the future of legal services and on the skills necessary to take advantage of the new emerging markets being opened by tech and innovation. Hersh is considered a valued mentor and advisor to dozens of legal tech startups and continues to connect with companies from around the world. Hersh previously served as chief of staff of Deloitte's Artificial Intelligence practice and spent five years at Queens Park as a senior advisor to several ministers; before that he spent a decade fundraising in the not-for-profit world. Sports, politics, and the lake are his passions and he enjoys them with his wife, two sons, and his dog Bauer.

Chris Bentley

Chris Bentley is the managing director of the Legal Innovation Zone (LIZ) and the Law Practice Program (LPP), both housed at Toronto Metropolitan University. Chris led the development of the LPP, a modern approach to lawyer licensing authorized by the Law Society of Ontario. He also co-founded LIZ, Canada's first incubator dedicated to legal startups, to help deliver better legal solutions to consumers. It supports legal startups; R & D for law firms, businesses, organizations, and government; and practical reform initiatives. Chris was elected as an Ontario MPP for London West from 2003 to 2013. He was a member of Cabinet for all ten years, serving as minister in five Cabinet posts: four years as attorney general, as well as Labour, Training Colleges and Universities, Aboriginal Affairs, and Energy. He drove a number of change initiatives, such as civil justice reform, the largest funding increase in Legal Aid's history, and was part of a new approach to indigenous relations recognized by the United Nations. For 23 years before politics, Chris practiced criminal defense and labor law. He taught part-time for ten of those years at Western's Law School.

Mary Juetten

Mary Juetten has dedicated her more-than-35-year career to helping individuals and businesses achieve and protect their success. Mary is a mediator, lawyer, and accountant who specializes in leading companies in transition or startup phases and helping create sustainable, operational, and financial growth. Using an undergraduate business degree from McGill and a JD and master's of law from Arizona State, as well as her U.S. and Canadian public accounting certifications, Mary created Trakight, the only self-guided software platform that creates a custom intellectual property (IP) strategy and assesses business risk plus generates leads and triages for companies, attorneys, mediators, and CPAs. In 2015, Mary co-founded Evolve Law and spoke internationally on change and technology adoption in the legal industry before selling the company to Above the Law. Mary was named to the American Bar Association's Legal Resource Technology Center 2016 Women in Legal Tech list and the FastCase Class of 2016. Mary is an international writer, blogger, speaker, mentor, and the author of

Small Law Firm KPIs: How to Measure Your Way to Greater Profits and *The Business of Legal: The Data-Driven Law Practice.* She currently serves on the Global Collaborative Law Council and teaches in the Suffolk Law legal technology certificate program.

Jim Calloway

Jim Calloway is the director of the Oklahoma Bar Association Management Assistance Program, where he has served for 24 years. He served as chair of ABA TECHSHOW 2005. He received his JD from the University of Oklahoma, where he was named to the Oklahoma Law Review. He publishes the award-winning law blog *Jim Calloway's Law Practice Tips* and co-authored three ABA books on law practice management. Mr. Calloway produces, with Sharon Nelson, the monthly podcast *The Digital Edge: Lawyers and Technology.* Mr. Calloway is a member of the Oklahoma Bar Association and the American Bar Association, where he is a member of the ABA Law Practice Division's Law Practice Magazine editorial board and wrote the practice management advice column for that magazine for five years. He was awarded the Law Practice Division's Robert P. Wilkens Award in recognition of Best Column in Division Publications in 2015. In 2018, he was awarded the William G. Paul Oklahoma Justice Award from Legal Aid Services of Oklahoma, Inc., for his work on access to justice projects. He has been inducted as a fellow of the College of Law Practice Management.

AJ Skogerson

AJ Skogerson is a lawyer, Collaborative Professional, mediator, educator, content creator, and consultant. She loves laughter, big ideas, and any kind of adventure, big or small. In 2017, AJ combined forces with attorney Andrea McGinn to co-found The Law Shop by Skogerson McGinn LLC—Iowa's first private practice law firm offering unbundled legal services to all clients. The Law Shop has quickly become a leader in helping to show the world that providing high-quality legal assistance on a limited-scope basis increases access to justice for all, while vastly improving the well-being of lawyers in a multitude of ways. AJ and Andrea present and provide workshops on unbundled legal services locally, regionally, and internationally.

The Law Shop has been featured in professional publications such as *The Iowa Lawyer, Illinois Bar Journal*, and the *ABA Journal*. With 20 years of experience working with clients, attorneys, judges, and courts as well as professional and community organizations, AJ strives to be a positive light and consistent source of help and encouragement for others.

Andrea McGinn

Andrea McGinn is an attorney and co-founder of The Law Shop by Skogerson McGinn LLC, a 100 percent unbundled legal services law firm in Van Meter, Iowa. Andrea and her husband Nick have two young boys who help to inspire Andrea's passion for helping children and families by practicing primarily in the areas of family and child welfare law. She is also chair of the Iowa State Bar Association Family and Juvenile Law Section as well as an active member and leader in organizations such as Iowa Collaborative Divorce, Iowa Association for Justice, International Academy of Collaborative Professionals, Iowa Domestic Violence Death Review Team, Iowa Child Protection Council, and other professional and community-based organizations. Andrea and her law partner AJ Skogerson regularly present and provide professional workshops as well as individual and group coaching on unbundled legal services. Andrea's drive for positive change in the world is revealed in the way The Law Shop strives to improve both access to justice and the personal well-being of other professionals working within the judicial system.

Ginevra Saylor

Ginevra Saylor is national director of Innovation and Knowledge Programs with the global law firm Gowling WLG LLP, where she leads the firm's innovation, knowledge management, learning and development, legal project management, client and practice solutions, and process re-engineering strategy and initiatives. In previous KM leadership roles with two major firms, Ginevra developed strategies and initiatives for innovation, knowledge management, client solutions, technology adoption, and process improvement, and designed new projects and practice tools to leverage and build her firms' knowledge base. A member of the Pennsylvania and

Ontario Bars, she also has extensive and varied past experience as a practicing litigator and educator. Ginevra currently serves as president of the International Legal Technology Association (ILTA) Board of Directors and is a College of Law Practice Management (COLMP) fellow. She and her Gowling project team won a 2021 Precedent Innovation Award for developing a contest rules application, and Ginevra earned the ILTA 2016 Publications Shining Star Award and the 2016 Global Knowledge Management Congress Knowledge Management Leadership Award. She is a frequent author and international speaker on legal practice, innovation, legal technology, knowledge management, and related topics.

Greg Siskind

Greg Siskind is a founding partner of Siskind Susser, PC—Immigration Lawyers, and has been practicing law since 1990. Greg began practicing law when he was 22, after receiving his bachelor's degree from Vanderbilt University and his law degree from the University of Chicago. Greg is the author of seven books and hundreds of articles and book chapters. He is also the author of a number of immigration-related pieces of legislation and has testified as an expert in front of the U.S. House of Representatives Immigration Subcommittee. In 1994, he created www.visalaw.com, the first immigration law firm website in the world. That same year, he began publishing *Siskind's Immigration Bulletin*, a newsletter that was the first electronically distributed law firm newsletter. The newsletter is still going out to tens of thousands of people every month. In 1998, he became the first lawyer in the world with a blog, and, in 2016, he became one of the first lawyers to begin publishing artificial intelligence immigration tools for both lawyers and consumers. He is regularly interviewed by publications like *USA Today*, *The Wall Street Journal*, *The New York Times*, *Time*, *The Washington Post*, NPR's *All Things Considered*, *Forbes*, and *Bloomberg*.

Lisa Feldstein

Lisa Feldstein is the principal lawyer at Lisa Feldstein Law Office PC. She is a health and fertility lawyer focused on a niche she calls Family Health Law™. She is also an adjunct professor at York University, where she teaches health care law in the Faculty of Health. In addition, Lisa previously taught negotiation at Osgoode Hall Law School. Lisa has been widely published, including in the *National Post*, the *Canadian Journal of Family Law*, *The Advocates' Quarterly*, and the *McGill Journal of Law and Health*. She wrote the reproductive law chapter in the textbook *Introduction to Health Law in Canada*, which was published in 2019 by Emond Publishing. Lisa is a regular presenter for universities, health care facilities, and community organizations. She has been featured by numerous media outlets, including Global News, CTV, *Vanity Fair*, *Macleans Magazine*, *Law Times*, and CBC. In 2015, she was honored to win a Precedent Setter Award for demonstrating excellence and leadership early in her practice. In 2020, Lisa founded Kinkeeper™, the access to justice branch of her firm that offers online courses for family caregivers. Lisa was recognized with a Precedent Innovation Award in 2022.

Jordan M. Atin

Jordan is a certified specialist in estates and trusts law and an adjunct professor of law at Osgoode Hall Law School in Toronto, Canada. Jordan is the co-creator of eState Planner (e-stateplanner.com), will planning software that is being used by more than 400 law firms in Ontario. He is a past chair of the Ontario Bar Association—Trust and Estates Section and a full member of the Society of Trusts and Estate Practitioners (STEP). Jordan was the inaugural winner of the OBA's Hoffstein Prize in recognition of his contributions and achievements in the area of wills, trusts, and estates. He is a frequent presenter and chair at STEP, Osgoode Hall Law School, Metropolitan Toronto Lawyers' Association, Ontario Bar Association, and Law Society programs on estate matters. Jordan is a contributing author to the well-known text "Estate Litigation" and his articles are referred to in many of Canada's leading estates texts, including *Widdifield on Executors and Trustees*, *Feeney's Canadian Law of Wills*, *Drafting Wills in Ontario*, and *Oosterhoff on Wills and Succession*. Jordan's book for non-lawyers, *The Family War—Winning the Inheritance Battle*, has been featured on CanadaAM, BNN, and in dozens of Canadian and U.S. newspapers.

Index